What people are saying about …

THE POWER OF BELONGING

'Belonging within a team has been at the heart of all my adventures: It has helped me make a home in some of the most hostile environments on the planet. I recommend *The Power of Belonging* to you as a great place to explore the security you need for leadership.'

Bear Grylls, adventurer

'Will van der Hart has an invaluable gift for helping us address areas of our lives where we have been hurt and broken – and to find our security in Jesus. He and Rob Waller show us that vulnerability is a strength which can enable us to flourish as leaders in the power of the Holy Spirit.'

Nicky Gumbel, leader
at HTB and Alpha

'*The Power of Belonging* is full of wisdom, insight, and common sense. In an age when many are crippled by insecurity, shame, and loneliness, the authors confront these issues boldly yet sensitively. They are honest and vulnerable, and this is what gives them their credibility. Not written from an ivory tower but in the midst of their own quest to lead from a place of belonging.'

Rev. Canon Mike Pilavachi, cofounder and leader of Soul Survivor

'Through their work with Mind & Soul, Will van der Hart and Rob Waller have enabled thousands to be heard and helped and to step into deep healing. I commend their work and especially this new book, *The Power of Belonging*. In a fickle world of fame and followers, this book is essential reading. We are "A" people: more anxious than ever before, crying out to be seen and matter at the deepest level. *The Power of Belonging* enables the reader to step free into truth, hope and substance.'

Beth Redman, author and songwriter

'In order to build well, we need solid foundations, but too many times our lives are built with fundamental fault lines that jeopardize what we are seeking to establish. This book explores the vulnerabilities that are so often concealed inside the fabric of our hearts and minds; challenging us to face them. Will and Rob invite us not just to read a book but to take a journey and discover the power of belonging. When we learn how to truly belong, we learn how to build truly.'

Charlotte Gambill, lead pastor
at Life Church UK, author,
and international speaker

'*The Power of Belonging* should be required reading for any leader who aspires to lead with integrity, fulfilment, and longevity. In this book, Will van der Hart and Rob Waller provide sound and timely advice: leadership can be very lonely and leaders can make unwise decisions when they forget that they belong. Will and Rob use the paradigm of Moses, the foremost figure of the pre-Christian world who took a race of slaves under inconceivable circumstances and led them into a mighty nation, and teach us unforgettable steps to belong and lead.'

Dr. Jerry Johnston, professor
of Theology at Houston
Baptist University

'*The Power of Belonging* is clever and witty, yet real and at times even raw. The authors venture into psychological territory where few leaders dare to tread. They embark upon a courageous journey through the corridors of vulnerability out into the open spaces of newfound freedom. This is a great read for those leaders ready to take a good, long, hard look in the mirror and envision a future beyond insecurities and fraudulent facades. Packed with personal illustrations and practical wisdom, readers are sure to be encouraged.'

Dr. Robi Sonderegger, clinical
director at Psychology Café
and Psychology Milk Bar,
Family Challenge Charitable
Trust, Australian Institute
of Clinical Psychology

'Will and Rob point us to the problem at the core of so much leadership turmoil—shame; and toward its solution—belonging. As a pastor I found *The Power of Belonging* immensely helpful in thinking through my own "shame story" and the impact it has on my leadership. It helped me come to terms with the degree to which my own emotional security and sense of relational belonging are tied to my leadership and the need to address these deeply personal issues if I am to lead well. This book is urgently needed in the current crisis of Christian leadership. In a climate where many "successful" Christian leaders are being derailed when their own internal dysfunction catches up with them, there is powerful wisdom here.'

Reuben Munn, senior pastor of Shore Community Church, New Zealand

THE

POWER

—*of*—

BELONGING

THE

Will van der Hart & Rob Waller

POWER

— *of* —

BELONGING

DISCOVERING THE CONFIDENCE
TO LEAD WITH VULNERABILITY

DAVID C COOK

transforming lives together

THE POWER OF BELONGING
Published by David C Cook
4050 Lee Vance Drive
Colorado Springs, CO 80918 U.S.A.

Integrity Music Limited, a Division of David C Cook
Eastbourne, East Sussex BN23 6NT, England

The graphic circle C logo is a registered trademark of David C Cook.

The website addresses recommended throughout this book are offered as a
resource to you. These websites are not intended in any way to be or imply an
endorsement on the part of David C Cook, nor do we vouch for their content.

Details in some stories have been changed to protect
the identities of the persons involved.

Unless otherwise noted, all Scripture quotations are taken from Holy Bible, New
International Version® Anglicised, NIV® Copyright © 1979, 2011 by Biblica, Inc.®
Used by permission. All rights reserved worldwide. Scripture quotations marked
ESV are taken from ESV® Bible (The Holy Bible, English Standard Version®),
copyright © 2001 by Crossway, a publishing ministry of Good News Publishers.
Used by permission. All rights reserved; THE MESSAGE are taken from THE
MESSAGE. Copyright © by Eugene H. Peterson 1993, 2002. Used by permission
of Tyndale House Publishers, Inc.; and NLT are taken from *Holy Bible*, New Living
Translation, copyright © 1996, 2007 by Tyndale House Foundation. Used by
permission of Tyndale House Publishers, Inc., Carol Stream, Illinois 60188. All
rights reserved. The authors have added italics to Scripture quotations for emphasis.

LCCN 2018952797
ISBN 978-0-8307-7593-4
eISBN 978-0-8307-7716-7

The Team: Ian Matthews, Amy Konyndyk, Nick Lee, Susan Murdock, Jo Stockdale
Cover Design: Mark Prentice at beatroot.media

Printed in the United Kingdom
First Edition 2019

1 2 3 4 5 6 7 8 9 10

100518

To those who long to belong.

CONTENTS

ACKNOWLEDGEMENTS

Rob would like to thank the Health Boards of Scotland and New . Zealand for their continued support. Will would like to thank the team at Holy Trinity Brompton for their ongoing encouragement. Special thanks to Dr. Jane Williams, Sarah Jane Shore, Abi Johnson, and Katherine Chow for their constructive reflections on the early scripts. We are hugely indebted to Antonia Miller for her brilliant illustrations and to Charlie Mackesy for his cartoon.

Deep thanks to the editorial and marketing teams at David C Cook for their skill and patience in working with our many drafts, and for sharing in our vision for this book, particularly to Ian Matthews and Jack Campbell. Special thanks go to Amy Boucher Pye as well. We would also like to thank everyone who has offered us their support and kindly written endorsements.

We are so thankful to Susanna and Lucinda (our wives), and to our families for their unwavering support, and to God to whom we radically belong.

INTRODUCTION

'Maybe the degree to which we belong anywhere isn't actually measurable. Maybe it's just a gentle onward movement.'[1]

Naomi Reed

Are you looking for ways to improve your leadership, increase your influence, or gain authority? All great leaders are great learners, constantly trying to improve the way they lead others, and yet most of the leadership training we receive is external to us: vision, communication, management, strategy. But what if the greatest gift to your leadership was already yours? What if the power that you need to reach a new dimension of leadership was actually lying under a dirty sheet in your own basement?

This book is a guide to enable you to uncover what we believe is already yours—the power of belonging. And yet this is not a simple journey: that dirty sheet is the shame that hides the most precious and powerful leadership message we will ever know. The basement is often bolted and locked, lest anyone else realise that we are not as wonderful as we would like them to believe. Our stories seem to point in the opposite direction—away from vulnerability and towards learned strength—and so we need to face reality before we find revelation. It is a struggle, but to uncover the reality of your belonging is to be transformed not just in your leadership, but in your life.

> (Will): My first church in North West London had a problem with what I call, 'Anglican Damp'; that sweet, mouldy smell that lingers in so many historic church buildings. Wanting to make the church as welcoming as possible, I set about trying my best to make the place smell better, and a toilet renovation project seemed like the logical place to start. However, even after installing brand-new loos, new flooring, and even air fresheners, the unwelcome damp smell persisted.
>
> About six months later, I had conceded that 'Anglican Damp' was likely to be with me throughout my ministry, when, walking around the exterior of the building, I came upon a small locked door. It took some serious persuasion to get the key from the maintenance man who had claimed that it 'wasn't worth opening'. But after exercising what little leadership I had, I found myself holding a stick in one hand and a torch in the other, ready to battle my way through the cobwebs.
>
> I was stopped abruptly after only two steps to find that the entire stairwell and basement beyond were completely flooded with putrid water. I notified the fire brigade, who later arrived on the scene to drain out the water. But even with their industrial pumps, it took over

five hours to clear. What remained was the rusty carnage of ninety years of stored camping equipment and miscellaneous church junk. This had been the source of all my suffering! 'Anglican Damp' wasn't an annoying but largely innocent smell; it was an indication that the whole building was flooded at its foundations!

Our work together is well illustrated by that flooded basement. Many leaders are plagued by a vague sense of fraudulence, unworthiness, or incompetence. They work tirelessly to improve the public-facing aspects of their life and leadership—renovating, polishing, and sprucing wherever possible. Yet, no matter how much effort they put in, or achievement they realise, the same feelings reappear.

According to the *Journal of Behavioral Science*, a sense of fraudulence is pervasive across our society. Impostor syndrome, as it is commonly known, affects approximately 70 percent of people at some stage of their lives.[2] Many reports suggest that it is particularly prevalent among people who are going through life transitions, such as students or those moving into new positions or phases of leadership. If you are battling impostor syndrome, you may recognise the symptoms: feeling trapped in a cycle of insecurity, performance, and defensiveness. An article by the American Psychological Association concludes, 'Often the people affected by impostor feelings don't realize they could be living some other way.'[3]

Ultimately this book seeks to take you on a journey with God through the locked door and into the shame basement in order that your sense of belonging might be restored and your leadership might be released from the grip of impostor syndrome.

WHAT COULD THE OUTCOMES BE?

(Will): A few months after our reclamation of the basement, a young man came up to me after church. He was newly married and said, 'Have you got anywhere in the church building that I can work out? My wife is really unhappy about me having all of my weights in our living room!'

I didn't skip a beat in offering him free access to our new rooms, now that they were dry and lit (although still slightly smelly). Over time, more people joined the work-out sessions. It became a huge comfort to me to know that early every morning a group of people were working out under our church building, listening to worship music and getting strong!

Our destination in *The Power of Belonging* is not just to drain the 'shame basement' but to turn it into an 'integrity gym'! This is a place of strength from which we can exercise our leadership confidently because we have established two tracks of belonging: firstly, that I belong within my spheres of relationship and leadership, and secondly, that I have secure and infinite belonging to God Himself.

Success on this journey will largely depend upon your openness to and engagement in the material that you read. The process of change will probably be painful and frustrating at times, but the benefits will make it worthwhile. We want to encourage you to risk the house for the sake of the home.

If you follow this path, we believe you are likely to see a positive impact in three areas of life:

Living Freely

For many people, shame (or a fear of shame) is a primary factor in their decision making. They live defensively to avoid humiliation or exert excessive control to mask their insecurity. Very soon these choices become automatic and are always heavily justified. Resolving shame enables you to make choices freely rather than under the threat of shame. At the heart of this freedom is a sense of true belonging, one that forms a foundation to healthy and unfettered decisions.

Loving Fully

The more life choices you make motivated by shame, the more you disconnect from your true self. This separation between the true self and the 'presented' self has a detrimental impact on relationships. Addressing your shame effectively enables you to accept and offer love—to welcome and celebrate those around you.

Leading Well

Resolving your shame could be the most powerful leadership decision you will ever make. You will move from leading from the margins to leading from the heart. Belonging undoes insecurities and defensiveness in leadership. It prophetically calls others to a place of authenticity and courage. Leaders who 'belong' create cultures that nourish others. They make the leadership journey a shared enterprise, not an independent activity.

TIPS FOR THE ROAD

This road is fraught with difficulties. Resistance to belonging will rise up within you as we address the bonds of shame. Shame cannot survive being called out—but doing so will involve taking the risk of being known. Shame cannot coexist with empathy—but embracing empathy will mean allowing ourselves to be loved. There is no need to 'bare all', but there is a need to be honest and open with yourself. Jesus warns us: 'Suppose one of you wants to build a tower. Won't you first sit down and estimate the cost to see if you have enough money to complete it?' (Luke 14:28). We need to enter this journey expecting some uncomfortable feelings and some unexpected realities. The cost of belonging is to carry the risk of rejection or humiliation. It is precisely because we want to avoid this cost that we lose the opportunity to lead securely; so make a commitment to the cost now and you will make great progress later on.

There is also a huge difference between knowing that something is true and allowing that truth to change your heart. You may put this book down because it is too challenging, but you are far more likely to read it through in a superficial way and nod in agreement without experiencing any life change. Shame-bound leaders are experts at deflecting anything that may engage with their shame, often without even realising it. They congratulate themselves for reading a book on shame and belonging, but the book's message bounces off the Teflon suit they wear.

Figure 1: Teflon leadership suit (not recommended).

With that reality in mind, we strongly recommend an active reading approach. Active reading involves a process of reading, engaging, reflecting, and applying. Each chapter ends with a study guide that includes exercises for your engagement and prompts for your reflection and that gives space for you to consider ways in which you can make direct application to your own life. We also believe God is on this journey with us—He is the 'alongside presence' and the 'wonderful counsellor' who can see the end of the road.[4]

There are other ways that you can read actively. You may choose to use this book as a small group study resource and work through it with a couple of trusted friends, or you may simply journal along with the text as important things come into your mind. The key point is that you allow this to be a personal journey rather than just an academic journey. This is a heart transplant, not a skin graft.

DEFEATED BY 'WHACK-A-MOLE'

(Rob): When I was growing up, the Scouts always had a Summer Fete. Going back to their Fete recently, I was amazed that some of the games I played forty years ago were still there and my own children enjoyed them.

One firm favourite over the years has been 'Whack-a-Mole' in which moles pop their heads out of a grid of holes. The goal is to take the rubber hammer and 'whack' the head of each mole before it disappears again. The activity gets more frenetic the more success you have until the moles are appearing and disappearing at such a rate that it is impossible to react quickly enough. My children usually end up exhausted and in fits of giggles, but inevitably defeated.

The search for belonging can be just like 'Whack-a-Mole' in which we try to defeat each obstacle to belonging as it shows its head. We hit appearance, career, social life, church activity, academic credentials ... We smash the inner blockages of worry, perfectionism, anger, guilt ... But no matter how many 'moles' we whack, our sense of un-belonging persists. We just end up exhausted and defeated.

This book is an attempt to unmask the mechanism that keeps the 'moles' from appearing because we need a deep solution that goes beyond the symptoms. This central mechanism is *shame*, a complex and often unaddressed emotion that we shall expose for what it is.

Shame-bound leaders appear 'nearly perfect' to those around them. They present brilliantly, work diligently, and serve humbly. They may even talk about community and authenticity. They don't look broken to those around them, but they are broken to themselves.

They may feel like frauds or suffer from low self-esteem and be plagued by embarrassment, defensiveness. They may suppress these feelings in activity and overwork but feel deeply lonely. They might even feel secure in the perceptions of others but not in their self-perception.

A PERSONAL JOURNEY

When you are setting out on something big, it is good to know who you are travelling with: The fact is that this is our journey too! We have written three books together—on worry, guilt, and perfectionism. They drew on our professional skills in theology and psychiatry. In those works, we disclosed that we struggled with these things and had found help in the techniques we shared. We like to think that we successfully hit a few of those moles pretty hard. But if we were absolutely real, we also wrote those books to put off writing this one!

It feels far too exposing of the fact that we sometimes haven't felt that we belonged, or fitted in. At times, we have lived and led with a sense of fraudulence and insufficiency that is exhausting and we have wondered what needs to change if we are going to live differently.

While accepting this fact feels humiliating enough, putting it on paper seems terrifying. Yet, it has also been our privilege to spend these last two years developing, researching, teaching, praying, and writing. This is our attempt to finally challenge the mechanism that keeps those moles from reappearing.

We also realise that we are not alone on this journey. The question of belonging is the question of our neighbours and our friends, our mentors and our pastors. It is a question asked in the high street, the gym, the shopping mall, and the church. It is a question that underpins all our work and relationships. It is a matter central to everyone's daily existence and eternal destiny.

The question of belonging doesn't only create a benign discomfort, but has a very active impact upon our decision making and leadership. We argue that our sense of positive 'belonging' has a transformational effect upon the quality of our leadership. It is our prayer that *The Power of Belonging* will be a significant part of your leadership formation and that it may play a part in raising up a generation of leaders who are not secretly bound by shame and feelings of fraudulence, but are liberated to lead well.

STUDY GUIDE: INTRODUCTION

How comfortable are you in your own skin? What do you worry about when no one is looking?

Do you identify with the need for a deeper solution to recurrent problems in your leadership? Which superficial things have you already addressed?

What is the most important outcome for you—living freely, loving fully, or living well? How do they relate to each other?

How would you describe your sense of belonging at the start of this journey? To what extent do you believe shame has limited it?

Chapter 1

LONGING FOR HOME

'The ache for home lives in all of us; the safe place where
we can go as we are and not be questioned.'[1]

Maya Angelou

(Will): I woke up from a fitful night's sleep in the
Appalachian Mountains, not sure whether it was the
altitude or the jet lag that saw me getting out of bed at
5:00 a.m. I had already planned the teaching I would
deliver to the church, whose weekend retreat I was
leading. Yet, rising in my mind was an odd question:
How do you pick up a snake? I got dressed and groggily
tramped out into the cold forest that surrounded my
lodge, prayerfully wondering what, if any, significance
this question had for my life.

It didn't take me long to recall the story of Moses' encounter with God at the burning bush. Far away from his home, Moses was hiding in the desert, living as a Midian shepherd. Then God appeared to him on Mount Horeb and called him into a leadership role that he felt desperately unqualified for.

Standing on top of my own mountain, far from my home in the UK, I sensed God was speaking to me. I often struggled with feelings of inadequacy for the calling on my life—I knew that fear was stopping me from addressing the snake-like shame issues in my life. I could hide behind the veneer of slick communication skills, but did God want my ministry to be about hiding or leading? Could I ever experience true belonging?

For the last two years, alongside my dear friend Rob, I have been studying the life of Moses and finding answers to questions that I never knew I needed to ask. This book is our journey to a sense of belonging in leadership that can best be described as 'feeling at home'. This can be your journey ...

STARTING FROM HOME

The best place to begin a journey to belonging is from the concept of 'home'. Defined as a place 'where one lives', home gives us the strongest impression of a place of authenticity, confidence, and freedom. It is a concept that we can all relate to even when our experiences of its reality are vastly different. To say, 'I feel at home here', is to express the greatest sense of security to lead. But what is 'home' to you—and how can you experience it within your leadership?

Psychotherapist and theologian Kent Hoffman describes a Circle of Security,[2] where 'home' has two functions, depending upon our needs. Firstly, it is a 'secure base' from which we can adventure into life. Secondly, it is a 'safe haven' to which we can return from the challenges of life. Without an image of home that can provide this sending and receiving, our leadership must stem from what we are currently doing. We place ourselves on our own pedestal and carve out a place in the world through our competence (or lack thereof). And we long for home.

> (Rob): I'm about as English as they come, with ancestors dating back to Saxon times. But twelve years ago, I moved to Edinburgh to marry my Scottish wife, and then two years ago, we moved as a family to New Zealand.
>
> My wife and I both have fond childhood memories of overseas homes (Jamaica and Mauritius, respectively) and wanted our two boys to experience something of the same. There was also an element of the 'travel bug'— perhaps making up for the adventures we never had, or because of the realisation that if we didn't go soon, it wasn't going to happen till the boys left home.
>
> Whilst we weren't consciously searching for home, the question of 'Whether and where have we felt at home?' is one that every traveller asks. We came to the strong realisation that home is a place in our hearts rather

than a place on the globe, and in the end, we made the decision to return to Scotland. Over the last couple of years, I have become more aware that my sense of belonging travels with me. It is found most clearly within my relationships with God, family, church, colleagues, and friends. This book is, in some ways, my journey.

IN THE ABSENCE OF HOME ... FAKE IT

The 'fake it to make it' cultural motto has grown up over recent years. It suggests that if you can pretend that you *feel* validated in what you are doing for long enough, you will eventually *be* validated and feel secure. But far more than a statement of strategy, this is often an exercise in confession. Our world is full of people who are faking their sense of belonging in the vain hope that when (or if) they 'make it', they will find validation. We feel anything but 'at home' but believe that if we pretend we do for long enough, the feeling will somehow suddenly show up.

> (Will): 'I have got no idea. Somewhere over there.' I pointed around the hillside as cold Welsh rain pelted down on our freezing bodies. I had a map and compass but had missed out on attending the orienteering training session and had no idea how to navigate to our destination.
>
> My group had passed the stage when it all feels 'a bit exciting' to be lost on the moors. Now they were in

the wet-and-cold incrimination stage. I had left their patience on a ridge ten miles back, and it was all grumbling and muttered threats at this point.

A call to Welsh Mountain Rescue was probably about an hour off when we finally fell through the door of the farmhouse that had been designated 'home'. My only comfort was the fact that the team were so exhausted and hungry they could barely voice their disdain for me publicly. I tried to make the best of it with comments like, 'Well we got there in the end!' But to be honest, there was no upside to this whole experience.

I was operating on the 'fake it to make it' principle in my orienteering adventure. What was I thinking? That I could fake reading a map long enough to finally get the hang of it and claim my new identity as a 'survivalist'? Even the most competent individuals can still feel insecure and fraudulent. No amount of skill, success, or wealth acquisition can generate a sense of authenticity, the security of home. This can only come from an understanding of your belonging.

Central to this book is the principle that authentic belonging makes for successful leadership. One example is found in outstanding sportspeople. Even in disciplines that appear to depend entirely on the skills of one individual, such as snooker or motor racing, winners will often point to their team as the reason for their success. In a post-race interview, Formula 1 world champion Lewis Hamilton said, 'I couldn't have done it without my team … This team is just remarkable and what we have achieved together is so special … These guys *also* did a great job.'³ Whether a tennis player or a pastor, business leader or a parent, a leader who truly believes that they belong finds a way to reach their fullest potential.

Many of the leaders who struggle with insecurity today started out by faking it. Initially their faux confidence seemed to work, but finding success in the eyes of those around them didn't make them feel more qualified; it just made them feel more fake! Carl Jung, the founder of analytical psychology, said, 'What was a normal goal for the young ... becomes a neurotic hindrance to the old.'⁴ In other words, people do whatever they can to climb up the career ladder in their younger years; the real struggle comes when they reach the top and realise that it's leaning against the wrong wall!

Figure 2: When you get to the top and realise you have been climbing the 'wrong wall'.

BROKEN HOMES

It is increasingly difficult to talk about 'home' in a manner that resonates positively with most people. It's not just that traditional nuclear families are becoming less common as much as the fact that the digital age has convoluted our experience of core relationships. We both grew up in small families, long before the Internet, mobile phones, and social media were easily accessible. Home was relatively defined by a fixed membership and a set of distinct values. Our parents both still live in their family 'homes'. Though such families are not guaranteed to have a sense of belonging, they do help to offer a vision of what home could be.

Your experience of 'home' may be wildly different. You may come from a broken home, have step-parents as well as parents, or have moved house often, maybe at critical times in your development. You may have even come from a 'home' in which love and security seemed entirely dependent upon your performance, behaviour, or achievements. If this is your experience, it can be harder to find a secure base and it is more tempting to hide your vulnerabilities.

The three books written by Veronica Roth in the Divergent series (made into films in 2014–16) tell of a dystopian future where people leave their families and enter 'factions' based on their personality and skills. The factions are meant to be home; 'stronger than blood and where you belong', but something in the system is not right. It takes one 'divergent' person who doesn't fit into a faction to bring the whole idea tumbling down and to show it for the oppression it is.

For many people, especially those in leadership, success appears to offer a form of 'home'. People around us, and on the Internet, react with approval to the achievements we present to them. Unfortunately, this model relies on our ability to replicate these success stories. It is called a news 'feed' because it gives rise to suppliers and consumers. We 'feed in' our news, and our reward is that our hunger for belonging is satiated for a while.

Yet when the news runs dry and there is no more genuine success to share, news gets replaced by fake news or people end up liking pictures of our evening meals.[5]

The Internet isn't the only place that encourages conditional belonging. Work and social environments can do this too; even supposedly accepting places like the church can feel conditional at times. In leadership, the standards for your belonging can feel even more rigorous and your vision of home can become hostile and dependent upon your latest performance.

It is for this reason that capturing a better vision of 'home' and a sense of belonging is so fundamental to establishing authentic leadership. If you don't know where you are coming from (sending) and what you are going to (receiving), there isn't much of a chance that you are going to get there or feel secure along the way.

THE YOUNG MOSES

Like many shame-bound leaders, Moses (from the early chapters of the Bible) was devoid of a secure model of home. Moses was born an exile slave during a period of particularly intense Egyptian oppression, only to be adopted into the house of Pharaoh follow-ing his rescue from the Nile.[6] These confused foundations had a significant impact on Moses' personal and leadership develop-ment, and yet they were also experiences that made him uniquely equipped for the mission to which God was to call him. Our work on belonging is assisted, not by denying our fragile foundations, but by acknowledging their impact on our lives: revelation always precedes restoration.

I imagine how a counsellor might have struggled to help Moses come to terms with his early home life:

…'Yes, Moses, I understand that it must have been hard being born into slavery whilst the Egyptians were seeking to kill your peers.'

…'I know, your mother did pop you in a basket when you were a baby and put you into a crocodile-infested river, but she had good intentions.'

…'Indeed, you were found by an Egyptian Princess, but I am sure she wasn't like her father at all. She was probably very kind.'

…'Yes, your mother pretended to be a midwife rather than admitting that she was your mother, but at least she got to spend time with you, Moses.'

…'I know, she ultimately handed you back to Pharaoh's daughter, but there really wasn't much more she could do.'

…'I think that's probably enough for this week, Moses …'

LEADERSHIP LONELINESS

Being without a home and feeling adrift is more than just an unpleasant emotion. It's dangerous, and we ignore it at our own peril. The fact is that in the absence of a positive vision of 'home', where we belong in healthy collaborative relationships, leaders naturally isolate themselves. They default into seeking the respect and admiration of others rather than looking to connect and collaborate. They dress this up with bullish statements like 'It's tough at the top!' and 'Leadership isn't for wimps', but isolation isn't a strength, or a sign of good leadership.

Figure 3: Leaders are good at hiding their loneliness.

Tough decisions sometimes have to be made in leadership, but they don't mean that a leader has to be devoid of real friendships, real collaboration, or a real sense of belonging. Indeed, the leaders who inspire us the most typically are those who have a reputation for good relationships as much as they do for great achievements. One example is Archbishop Desmond Tutu from South Africa. It is not just that Tutu is full of virtue in the task; he is overflowing with joy in its outworking, and this joy infects others. I (Will) was once privileged to be part of an interview with him, and I would guess that at least half of the interview was spent listening to him laughing! In his book *No Future without Forgiveness*, he writes about a term called *ubuntu*:

> A person with *ubuntu*[7] is open and available to others, affirming of others, does not feel threatened that others are able and good for he or she has a proper self-assurance that comes from knowing that he or she belongs in a greater whole and is diminished when others are humiliated or diminished, when others are tortured or oppressed.[8]

Some recent American research pooled many different studies on loneliness and found that being in healthy social relationships decreased mortality by around 50 percent—the same as giving up cigarettes. Being thin as opposed to obese gave you a 30 percent edge, and treating hypertension gave you 10 percent. To put it another way, loneliness is as bad for you as smoking and five times as bad as not taking your blood-pressure pills.[9]

Loneliness is not the same as being alone. Indeed, being alone and learning to be comfortable with solitude is a key marker of maturity and having a sense of home.[10] The loneliness we experience in leadership is often felt most keenly in the company of crowds of people; it's that we feel completely unknown by those around us and unable to allow ourselves to be known lest we are judged and found wanting.

HOMESICKNESS

One of the greatest challenges of leadership is working (or living) in an environment that does not feel supportive. Leadership is often exciting and pioneering, but it can leave us sick for something more familiar and encouraging. Leaders can survive in these environments for a season, but at a point it begins to make them sick for something that feels more like home. It's a bit like climbing Mount Everest: failure to become 'at home' on the mountain puts you at significant risk. If you cannot acclimatise, you cannot climb, let alone lead.

When we enter a new leadership environment, particularly one that is isolating, it can equally seem like the clock is ticking on our survival. It can feel like a 'make it a home or die' type experience where death is a slow and emotional one rather than anything more dramatic! Many leaders have been working without a 'sense of home' for years. Without belonging-based relationships they have become more vulnerable to shame and ironically more likely to isolate themselves. This puts them at risk of emotional suffering, but it also makes them devoid of the power that comes from knowing that they belong. One article on impostor syndrome by NBC comments, 'This cycle can quickly become an exhausting one, and has plenty of negative implications on not only your career, but your health, well-being and personal relationships.'[11] It's not that working in these environments is wrong—it's often a result of God's calling that we find ourselves there—but what we need to do is to find our home on these mountains and in these deserts of leadership.

(Will): After I left school at age eighteen, I spent a year working in a remote boarding school. I was really nervous about living away from home for the first time and wasn't sure how I would cope.

When I arrived, I was sent to my living quarters which were in an isolated building that stood in a field a mile away from the main school. I was told that I had a room to myself on the ground floor but later found that the supposed 'preparations' for my arrival had been overlooked. I stood on the threshold of my 'new home'. Furniture was piled up in the centre of the room, dust and cobwebs lay everywhere, and curtains hung limply by one or two remaining hooks. Thirty seconds after opening the door, tears were streaming down my face and I just wanted to get back into my car and begin the seven-hour return drive home.

I prayed through the sobs and then imagined what my mum would do, which would have been to separate the furniture she wanted from the junk and then begin washing everything! For an eighteen-year-old boy, this was a very new experience, but it was also strangely familiar. Establishing my vision of 'home' wasn't so much about how the room looked but about having the courage to establish the threads of my belonging in a new space.

The journey to belonging requires the courage to recapture a vision for our leadership where we 'feel at home', where we can be real and experience the support, acceptance, and compassion of those around us. The greatest mistake we can make on this journey is to assume that belonging is a passive or coincidental reality.

Neither is this about a failure to grow up. We can recreate aspects of the home we once knew, and there is nothing wrong with having familiar things around us. But if that is all it is, it becomes nostalgia—a wistful longing for what once was and we wish was the case again. Belonging is about establishing a vision of 'home' that is more than just historic.

Figure 4: Carrying a vision of home with us.

As Christians, we are called 'on' to a new home with a new birth (which some call being born again).[12] We are 'homesick' in the sense that we are currently between these two homes, but not in the sense that we want to turn back the clock. It is a longing for our home in Christ that pulls us forward, desiring this as a bridegroom desires his bride. From Alpha to Omega, from First to Last, from the Beginning to the End (Revelation 22:13), we are held and known.

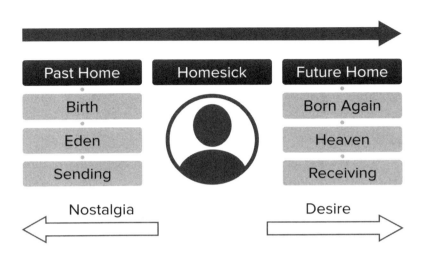

Figure 5: We are on a journey between two homes.

In John 20:21, the resurrected Jesus appeared to His disciples and said, 'Peace be with you! As the Father has sent me, I am sending you [out into the world].' The peace of God is present in sending as much as it is in arriving. It was the security of God that sent Jesus into the most hostile place, and now the security of Jesus was going with the disciples. They carried the foundations of 'home' with them into hostile and unknown environments, into places they often faced alone. The peace of God enabled them to do this because it was both their sending 'secure base' and their receiving 'safe haven'.

BELONGING AND UN-BELONGING

You may have heard of the Christian idea that we are 'in the world but not of it'. It's good to remember our Christian identity when we see destructive and unhelpful things around us, but this kind of thinking can leave us just as adrift as a leader with no real relationships. After all, what is the point of putting down roots here if we cannot call this 'home,' at least for now? Some Christian groups have taken this to an extreme level by never getting any insurance and not investing in a pension—and sadly, they have suffered the expected consequences.

This theology of 'radical un-belonging' can lead to one of three responses: separatism (go and find a cave), living in dualism (Sunday doesn't talk to Monday), or abandoning your Christian principles altogether (because this tension is intolerable). But the 'good news' is not of radical un-belonging; it's quite the reverse.

The courage required to belong is a spiritual discipline. It is good *now*, and not just in the future. We may be homesick, but this is a positive force that keeps us in that tension of knowing both where we have come from and where we are heading. We are both sent and received. We have both a secure base and a safe haven to which we are being drawn.

John 1:14 says, 'The Word became flesh and made his dwelling among us.' *The Message* version is phrased, 'The Word became flesh and blood, and moved into the neighbourhood.' It wasn't that the Word didn't belong; He belonged more than infinitely anything that He had created. It was His right to move in. God is not calling Christians to sit alone on the benches of life but to belong radically in the world that He made—to really 'dwell', not just to say, 'I am just passing through, so don't look to me for anything. I don't really live here; I am just waiting for heaven.'

Powerful leadership is rooted in belonging now, having a kingdom vision of home that is both present and future focussed.

We will refer to a 'belonging-based relationship' throughout this book. This is a relationship which is substantial beyond our 'usefulness to others'. It is a relationship within which we can describe ourselves as 'at home', secure in the knowledge that it will withstand our own shortcomings. Belonging-based relationships are ones that allow us the ability to be authentic and lead with vision and courage: to be who we really are, without fear.

Belonging-based relationships are not necessarily 'loving' or highly emotive. They can be experienced in the workplace, church, local community, or professional environment. They are as much a product of our own decision as they are something to be 'found' outside of ourselves. Our ambition is that you will have two tracks of belonging-based relationships from which to exercise your leadership: one that is held within authentic interpersonal relationships, and the other that is rooted in your relationship with God.

ALMOST BELONGING

You may have got this far in the book and thought 'this doesn't apply to me.' You are trying to be authentic; you don't feel lonely and aren't faking it—you've made some real sacrifices. However, you suspect we may be on to something as you don't feel sent from a secure base, nor do you feel that you have a safe haven to return to.

Leaders who 'almost belong' are usually doing great things, but they still carry a sense that this is an incomplete or inferior version of their 'real' calling. They have enough good things going on that they don't want to 'rock the boat' and they feel that they should be satisfied, and yet there is this longing for something greater.

Before Moses spent forty years shepherding the Israelite nation through the wilderness to the Promised Land, he shepherded the sheep of Midian in the desert for forty years. It was here that God met him in the burning bush and called him to change direction, returning to his original home in Egypt. It wasn't that he was apparently unhappy as a shepherd; it was that he was tending the wrong flock.

Moses' journey from shepherd of sheep to shepherd of people was the journey from un-belonging to belonging. It was the realisation of a true vision of 'home' in which all of his insecurities and doubts were recalibrated. God hasn't called us to 'almost belong'. He has called us to 'radically belong'; to lead in the confidence of knowing that we are His sons and daughters.

RADICAL BELONGERS

The theology of radical *belonging* is the discipline of knowing that you belong to God and therefore you belong in His world. The calling to love your neighbour is second only to loving God Himself. The only good neighbours are the ones who know that they belong—they belong despite all of the difference they see between those whom they live alongside.

It seems no coincidence that Jesus identified a Samaritan (loathed by his Jewish audience) to be the example of a good neighbour in Luke 10. His belonging wasn't limited by his ethnicity, geography, or social perception. It was the kingdom threads of home (of compassion, tenderness, courage, and godliness) that made his belonging authentic, even in a hostile place.

In a film about Jean Vanier (the founder of the L'Arch Communities), Vanier speaks tenderly to a young man with severe disabilities. 'You are so beautiful, Sebastian,' Vanier repeats as he holds the man's hand. There is not an ounce of insincerity in Vanier's words. He speaks with the conviction of a person who knows that he 'radically belongs' and is therefore able to offer a radical welcome to someone whom others may easily overlook.[13]

Vanier has spent his life establishing environments of 'home' for people who have been rejected by traditional society. He writes that 'community is not an ideal; it is people. It is you and me. In community, we are called to love people just as they are with their wounds and their gifts, not as we want them to be.'[14]

Vanier is a radical belonger, part of a group of extraordinary people who carry such a deep sense of 'home' that they have been able to radically love others. This radical belonging enables the individual to step beyond the petty competition that so often inhabits our relationships. People who 'radically belong' have no need for self-promotion because their insecurities about belonging are resolved. Their energy and intention are focused on their true mission.

JESUS THE RADICAL BELONGER

We see the ultimate radical belonger in Jesus Christ. Isaiah 53:3 gives us the context into which Jesus was called: 'He was despised and rejected by mankind, a man of suffering, and familiar with pain. Like one from whom people hide their faces he was despised, and we held him in low esteem.' Despite being born into the setting of rejection, Jesus carried the perfect state of belonging within Him.

We can read the New Testament with complete amazement. Amazement not just at the miracles of Jesus, but at the security and confidence He sustained at the points of highest pressure.

Often when Jesus performed a miracle, He asked those involved to remain silent.[15] Consider that for a moment; you have just raised a child from the dead and you ask for secrecy! The un-belonging in most of us would scream out, 'This is perfect. Now people are going to like me, welcome me, respect me, listen to me. Which social media channel would be best to utilise for this story to have the maximum reach?'

It is one thing to persistently refuse to seek the popularity of the crowd, but Jesus was also silent in His own defence. When He was tried before Pilate, the Bible says, 'Jesus remained silent.'[16] Silent! Put us in the same scenario, and our fear of rejection (let alone the impending pain and execution) would have had us flowing with expert testimony, denials, miracles ... anything to stop the outcome.

Jesus is the ultimate radical belonger because He has the ultimate relationship of belonging within Him. He knows that He is God's Son and that God is 'well pleased' with Him; He knows that He has 'everything under his feet'; and He knows that He will be there at the end.[17]

A VISION OF BELONGING

For many Christian leaders, the theology of 'radical un-belonging' often takes such a hold that no progress can really be made until they have a vision of something better. Reflections on radical belongers like Vanier give us a vision of the power and virtue of belonging. To know that we are capable of a profound depth of love when we are secure in our belonging to Christ can be a great motivation to us. Instead of seeing radical belongers as a saintly breed of individual who we can admire from a lowly distance, we can be released to the joy of loving without exchange—to lead securely and love unconditionally.

In our insecure states, however, we have very little time for Jesus' instruction in Matthew 5:44, 'Love your enemies and pray for those who persecute you.' It's not that we want revenge on our enemies. Far from it. We just don't have the security in our own belonging to know what it would even look like to love them. Uncovering the limitations of un-belonging in our lives and knowing the belonging that Jesus offers can radically transform our capacity to lead others well.

STUDY GUIDE: CHAPTER 1

Can you think of times when you have felt lonely or homesick? List these below.

Are you aware of the two 'homes' we live between? Which threads of your historic home and spiritual home would you want to live in today?

How do stories of radical belongers like Vanier or even Jesus make you feel? Are you in awe of them, seeing them as 'distant saints', or do they give you a vision of what is possible?

To what extent do you identify with 'almost belonging'? Which aspects of your current leadership practice do you think could be 'shadow mission' rather than 'true mission'?

Chapter 2

BELONGINGNESS

'A deep sense of love and belonging is an irreducible need of all people. We are biologically, cognitively, physically and spiritually wired to love, to love and to belong.'[1]

Brené Brown

(Will): I opened the email and read it with a growing sense of excitement: I had been invited to a leaders' retreat at Windsor Castle. The retreat was for a small group of younger leaders who were doing work that had some national significance. Our work within mental health and the church was growing and this invitation seemed like confirmation that we were having a positive impact.

However, my excitement quickly turned to discomfort and self-doubt. I started to think about others who would also be attending; leaders I really respected. 'I don't belong here' was the next thing that ran through my head, followed by a whole raft of doubts: *Did they really mean to invite me? Did someone else drop out?*

I couldn't escape the feeling that there had been a mistake and that the whole experience would be humiliating. Despite how irrational it was, I arrived at the castle early just to check I was actually on the list. Even having been invited in, I was still anticipating someone escorting me off the premises before the event even started.

I sat at the back of the first session, looking around the room at people that I admired. I kept thinking, *Why am I here?* Then the retreat leader said, 'There probably isn't a leader in this room that doesn't feel like a bit of a fraud, but let's just get over ourselves and worship Jesus.' I couldn't believe what I was hearing, but looking around the room, I saw many leaders nodding in agreement. I thought I was the only one who believed that they didn't really belong; but it was a common feeling amongst leaders who were doing things that I felt justified their presence far more than my own.

Whether it is within a leadership group, a sports team, community group, or a church, or amongst professional colleagues, a school class, or even a family, belonging tends to define whether or not we are having a positive experience of community. The challenge of belonging is that we are typically poor at assessing if we belong or not. The sense that 'I don't really belong here' erodes our confidence to lead more than any belief about our material competences. The feeling of un-belonging is also something that we tend to believe is unique to us, but it is in fact far more common than we think.

This desire and need to belong is a theme that runs through all cultures and throughout all time. Becoming aware of the impact of belonging on your leadership, and taking the steps to reappraise your sense of belonging, will have a transformational impact upon the way you lead.

BELONGINGNESS AS A FUNDAMENTAL MOTIVATION

Psychology is constructed out of building blocks—core drivers like the need for safety and warmth and food that you might have heard described in something called Maslow's Hierarchy of Needs.[2] The idea behind Maslow's hierarchy, proposed in 1943, is that you can't develop the finer skills further up the hierarchy (like self-esteem) until you have the basics sorted. To put it another way, you don't tend to worry about your social performance when someone is chasing you with a large knife.

Traditionally, only the bottom two levels have been seen as 'fundamental'—that is, essential for anything resembling normal life. Whilst the higher levels are desirable, it is clear that many people do not have social stability or self-esteem or self-actualization but manage to lead active lives that help others. However, newer developments in psychology have suggested that the need to belong (belongingness) is perhaps more fundamental than we thought—perhaps to the extent of it being as powerful a motivator as the need to eat, be warm, and to rest.

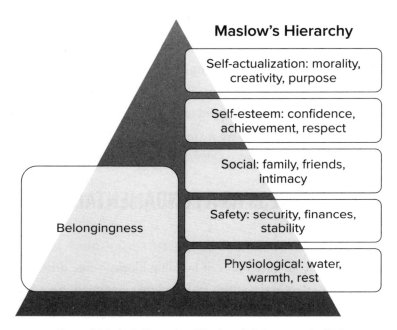

Figure 6: Maslow's Hierarchy of Needs with 'belongingness' added.

In 1995, psychologists Roy Baumeister and Mark Leary wrote a paper called 'The Need to Belong' in which they proposed that 'a need to belong is a *fundamental* human motivation ... that human beings have a pervasive drive to form and maintain a minimum quality of lasting positive and significant interpersonal relationships.'[3]

They argue that belongingness is worthy of this status because it meets certain criteria. People invariably form relationships even when under duress. This in turn affects their emotions, thoughts, and behaviours. It is seen across all cultures, and it also has a satisfaction point—when you have 'enough' belonging and don't need to seek more.

To put 'belongingness' plainly, you could say that we are created for connection. Belongingness is a means of describing the energy and motivation that we carry to build a connection with others. Think about the lengths that we go to for the sake of satisfying our need to connect and be reassured that we belong. There are the obvious examples, such as travelling vast distances just to be with loved ones at Christmas, right through to the subtleties of speech, dress, and social clues that demonstrate that we are part of a group. As Baumeister and Leary say, 'Much of what human beings do is done in the service of belongingness.'

Perhaps the reason that 'belongingness theory' seems to click is that it makes sense of some of the more ridiculous things we have done to fit in: from strange haircuts and fashions to feigning interest in certain bands (that we didn't even like!). Belongingness can even motivate us to push through physically painful experiences if we believe that they may lead to deeper relationships:

(Will): One Easter I spent nine days working in Guernsey. On the night I returned home, I was supposed to attend a dinner party hosted by my girlfriend's (now wife's) best friend, but I went down with the most terrible virus. Still feeling horrific, I flew back to the UK. Not only did I want to keep my girlfriend, I also wanted to impress her young and trendy friends.

I showered, then put on my best clothes, took some paracetamol, and grimaced my best smile. It was a wonderful party but probably the most uncomfortable I can remember. In my viral state, food made me nauseous. I forced my way through three courses, laughing and joking along with the conversation. As soon as it seemed appropriate to leave, I made my excuses and rushed around to my friend's flat where I was violently sick in his bathroom. I barely moved for the next two days!

FINDING MY HOME
City and Tribe

In the Old Testament, the nation of Israel is given a strong national identity. The Israelites have clear roles, such as caring for the less fortunate in their midst and being a light to the Gentiles. Different tribes have special roles, and when they settle in the land of Canaan, cities are built to make homes. Some cities are likened to Babylon (a pagan city, known for exile and slavery), but Jerusalem is a place of belonging, a precursor to the 'New Jerusalem' of heaven.[4]

Church and Community

In the New Testament, the focus switches from nation to the community[5] of believers—who are linked by faith rather than genetics. When people get together, there are always issues, but this does not mean that we are to avoid striving to make things work. In the book of Romans, Paul gives us eleven chapters of dense theology before poetically throwing his hands in the air at the inadequate words he has written (Romans 11:33–36) and then launching into four chapters on how to do relationships (chapters 12–15) and then one final chapter (16) giving twenty-three ties of belonging! As Nicky Gumbel says, 'Your belonging can only be found in the body of Christ.'[6]

Relationships

The Bible is underpinned by the value of loving human relationships. In Genesis 2:18, we are told, 'It is not good for the man to be alone,' and a partner is made for him, to be one flesh, to leave parents and belong together. Homes and families are created; new life is formed. Jesus tells us in Matthew 22:30 that in heaven people 'will neither marry nor be given in marriage.' This is partly because (theologically) we will see the ultimate marriage of Christ and His bride (the church), but also (because of belongingness) we will feel God's love so clearly that we will not need other relationships in the same way. Until that time, human relationships are a vehicle through which we can sense our belonging, both to each other and in part to God (the two tracks of belonging).

Heaven

All of the above are foretastes of heaven. Our citizenship is in heaven,[7] not in nations or tribes. We will 'dwell with God' and He will 'wipe away every tear from [our] eyes.'[8] Jesus tells us that His Father's house has many rooms and He has gone there to prepare them for us.[9]

Heaven is the theological conclusion of our search for belongingness. People have many definitions of heaven, but common to
most of them is the idea that it will be a big party with all your
favourite people there—a place where we will finally belong for
eternity.

If we are not careful, though, over-focussing on heaven can
lead to a paradoxical 'non-belonging' form of faith where we long
for heaven so much we never really live on earth! Christian leaders
are particularly at risk of developing a 'bunker mentality' where the
hardship of isolated leadership is seen as a trade-off against heaven's
community bliss.[10] Whilst escape may at times be welcome, this is
not the biblical pattern; neither is it good for our leadership.

We are called to be the best leaders we can be for the sake of
Jesus, informed by the promise of heaven and the love of God for His
broken and hurting world. Invariably leadership that is informed by
heaven will be informed by belonging. Scripture talks about renewal
and restoration, and gives us many avenues for belonging and living
together—starting now!

BELONGING YET NOT BELONGING

With so many reasons to want and need to belong, it seems cruel
that so many feel they don't. They know that technically they are
part of something—a family, a church, a football club—but the *feeling* of belonging is not there. If you look back to the hierarchy of
needs figure earlier in the chapter, you will see that belongingness is
not the same as the presence of family, friends, or sexual intimacy.
It is a more basic need—to *feel* that you belong—and this almost

needs to be present before you can make anything of your social opportunities.

Marriage is a good example of this. If two very broken people get married, that marriage is unlikely to be the solution to their issues. Instead, it will highlight these even more as their neediness gives rise to mistrust, fear of openness, and feeling alone, even though they are sharing a bed. Actor Robin Williams said, 'I used to think that the worst thing in life was to end up all alone. It's not. The worst thing in life is ending up with people who make you feel all alone.'[11]

Which of the following situations do you identify with? Would you say that one of them is a core issue for you that has implications for many parts of your life?

- I am part of this family, but I am not loved by this family
- I belong in this school, but I am bullied in this school
- I am a member of this church, but I feel un-accepted in this church
- I am joined in marriage, but I am rejected in my marriage
- I am with my friends, but I am unknown by my friends
- I am a co-worker, but I am not trusted as a colleague

This might have been how Moses felt as a young man—an Israelite but living in his 'home', the Egyptian palace.

The Bible story doesn't give us much detail about Moses' adolescence, but it is sensitively considered in the 1998 DreamWorks retelling *The Prince of Egypt*.[12] Having seen a visual depiction of the Hebrew massacre on the temple walls, the young Moses challenges Pharaoh Seti, who responds, 'Oh my son ... they are only slaves.'

Pharaoh uses possessive and paternal language, undermining Moses' true racial identity. Moses is to Pharaoh both 'my son' and 'not my son, living in my house but not of my house'.

Inevitably Moses felt he didn't truly belong. When he killed the Egyptian slave driver in Exodus 2:12, he didn't even consider that the forgiveness of Pharaoh might be available to him. (Pharaoh tried to kill him in verse 15—a sign of how little Moses truly belonged in the Royal Court.)

THE SOCIOMETER

Within our brains, we have a very complex mechanism which responds to social threats. Because belongingness is so precious, it has a good alarm system. This 'sociometer' continually evaluates our social position and its possible impact on our belonging. You might imagine the sociometer is a bit like a mirror: we aspire to look good and we use the mirror to either confirm or deny that we have achieved our ambition. Unfortunately, the mirror is only as objective as we are: if we over-scrutinise what we see, we are likely to believe we have failed to meet our desired standard.

(Will): Recently, I checked the mirror at work midway through the morning. Only then did I realise that I had commuted into my office with a stream of baby sick down my shoulder. I immediately cleaned my jumper with tissues and soap, not because my baby's sick offended me, but because it might have led people to withdraw from me or caused them embarrassment.

Until a few hundred years ago, shameless behaviour could be life threatening. Exile from the community could mean exclusion from heat, light, shelter, food, relationship, and protection. To be 'cast out' or an 'outcast' could literally be a life sentence. It is not surprising, then, that we have developed such a powerful mechanism to monitor the threats to our belonging.

However, the sociometer can become incorrectly calibrated. If we don't have a deep sense of security and belonging, then we can interpret incidents as socially threatening and shaming even when the trigger is not that large. This, in turn, can constantly undermine our desire to belong at all.

Figure 7: The sociometer often gives us a false reading of the likelihood of rejection.

(Will): One Sunday during 'The Peace' (a time of greeting in the Anglican Church), a congregation member reached out her hand to me (the vicar). Having not seen this gesture of friendship behind me, I warmly greeted those to my left and right.

After the service, she hurried away, and it was several weeks before I realised there was a serious problem. I asked her in for a conversation with me, and when she explained what had happened, I apologised profusely for having not seen her. However, I could tell that she did not really believe that my slight had been unintentional and she was possibly even more offended that I had 'not seen her' in the first place.

As a result, her trust in me was diminished, and after another perceived rejection by a different member of the congregation, she left the church.

You can see from this experience how an individual's shame story can establish a path of inevitability in life. In each apparently new circumstance, the hypersensitivity to being shamed further folds into a new humiliating experience. The sociometer is trying to defend the individual from rejection, and instead it finds rejection where there is none. Gradually a person creates such powerful defences against future shaming experiences that they drive away belonging-based relationships.

INTRODUCING SHAME

When the sociometer fails to find belonging and anticipates rejection, a person experiences shame. Whilst guilt is negative feelings about our actions, shame is negative feelings about ourselves. Gershen Kaufman wrote, 'Shame is the most disturbing experience individuals ever have about themselves; no other emotion feels more deeply disturbing because in the moment of shame the self feels wounded from within.'[13]

We want to conclude this chapter with a recap of the very real connection between belonging and shame:

1. We all carry a fundamental human motivation to belong in relationships.

2. We estimate our belonging through a subjective 'sociometer'.

3. When we believe we belong, we experience positive emotions, increased confidence, and authority to lead.

4. When we estimate rejection or humiliation, we experience negative emotions, primarily shame.

5. A sense of belonging motivates us to invest more deeply in belonging-based relationships.

6. A sense of shame motivates us to isolate ourselves from others and defend against further rejection.

STUDY GUIDE: CHAPTER 2

Do you agree that 'belongingness' is a fundamental human motivation, like hunger and fear? Why, or why not?

Are you part of a relationship, a church, or other community? Do they make you feel at home? If so, how? If not, what could you do to help build this feeling?

Are you prone to check your sociometer on a regular basis? Does assessing other people's acceptance make you feel more secure?

Do you agree that shame is the main enemy of belonging? What is your first memory of feeling excluded?

Chapter 3

UNDERSTANDING SHAME

'Our sense of belonging can never be greater
than our level of self-acceptance.'[1]

Brené Brown

A PROBLEM WITH OUR FOUNDATIONS

It took about six months for the 'Anglican Damp' smell—that I (Will)
discussed in our introduction—to completely disappear from our
church building. You can imagine the conversations that followed my
discovery of the flooded basement, which centred on how long ago the
basement had been checked for leaks.

Just like 'Anglican Damp', shame is largely nondescript, but it
influences us in subtle, barely perceptible ways. If we do become
consciously aware of shame, we likely attribute it to other more obvious problems in our lives. These are things that fall more naturally
within our sight line: issues in our jobs or relationships that we find

mildly humiliating or frustrating. We may deal with these things competently, but no amount of tinkering on the surface (or 'whacking moles') will impact the huge problem under the floorboards.

Many of us do a reasonable job of creating an inspirational persona from which we exercise our leadership. But if our flooded foundation issues haven't been addressed, we will be plagued by the sense that we don't belong in leadership. The result is that we don't lead out of security towards success, but that we seek out success to find our security. If we haven't addressed the shame that inhibits our belonging, no amount of success will make us feel secure in ourselves or our leadership.

WHAT IS SHAME?

We find it easy to describe some emotions, such as sadness or anxiety, even if our experiences are specifically individual. Shame, however, like water in the basement, is particularly problematic to conceptualise, and as a result, it is often left unaddressed. You can worry or be a perfectionist or say, 'I am guilty,' but try to apply these ideas to shame and nothing works: I shame, be a shame, I am shame …! The best we can do is say, 'I feel ashamed.' But what does shame actually feel like?

THE SHAME CONDUCTOR

Imagine a full orchestra of ninety musicians. We can split the orchestra into four core parts: woodwind, brass, percussion, and strings. Which of these do you think is the most powerful? The tuba maybe, or perhaps the timpani drums? Now, what if we split our own emotional orchestra in the same way? According to the University of Glasgow, we would have four groups of emotions: happy, afraid (surprised), sad, and angry (disgusted).[2] In your experience, which of these is the most powerful?

The fact is that the most powerful instrument in an orchestra is not the drums or the tuba; it is the conductor's baton. The only instrument amongst the ninety represented by the orchestra that doesn't make a sound has control over everything.

Figure 8: The 'shame conductor' distorts our emotions.

Likewise, shame can be the most powerful instrument in our emotional orchestra. Psychologist Silvan Tomkins talks about the 'primacy of affect', meaning that shame is a powerful state that can conduct our emotions.[3] Despite its subtlety, or 'not having a sound of its own', shame can bring a fearful tone to a happy experience or a sense of disgust to a proud moment.

The conductor of an orchestra may choose to give priority to only certain instruments. Once the orchestra has been playing under the direction of a particular conductor for some time, it begins to respond automatically to the musical style in which it has been directed. There's always too much brass and never enough wood-wind, for example.

Shame-based responses can become learned and automatic behaviours, whilst we may remain unaware of the huge impact they are having on our leadership. We may even be reluctant to identify them for fear of making things worse. You don't need to dismiss the orchestra to change the music; but change the conductor and you will find that things sound infinitely better.

TWO SURFACE TYPES

Shame manifests upon a scale between two seemingly opposite social styles. Some people are visibly ashamed, shy, and socially anxious. Others seem to be in perfect social control—but underneath feel wildly out of their depth, unworthy, and unacceptable. These two groups are what we call the socially anxious and the socially controlled.

The Socially Anxious

Shame is closely linked to embarrassment and the idea of social anxiety—a fear of social situations such as parties, public speaking, and confrontation.

Socially anxious people worry about saying something foolish or being somehow found out. Bodily symptoms of anxiety such as sweating and shaking can occur. They anticipate rejection and worry about situations in advance or do a 'post-mortem' afterwards to check they did okay—often picking up threats that don't exist. Unhelpful coping mechanisms, like using alcohol or avoiding eye contact, can make the situation worse.

People with social anxiety 'get by' with a range of what psychologists call 'safety behaviours', such as always having to carry a bottle of water around in case their throat is dry. This means the social anxiety grumbles on at a low level and the issue is never fully dealt with; they never learn that this is 'just the anxiety talking'.[4]

This is especially true with leaders, because leadership invariably involves social situations and usually the requirement to perform. Leaders may be so anxious during such events that they miss out on other parts of their role. If you are focused inwardly on yourself as someone who fears being humiliated or rejected, you will not be able to tell how your talk, pitch, or sermon has gone down with those listening.

The story of Moses illustrates his struggle with social anxiety. He was asked by God to go and speak to Pharaoh, but on three occasions (Exodus 4:10, 6:12, 6:30), he gave 'slow speech' and 'faltering lips' as excuses not to. God graciously came up with a pragmatic solution—his more eloquent brother Aaron would be the mouthpiece—but Aaron became a safety mechanism for Moses, meaning his worries about public speaking persisted. His preoccupation with being humiliated and looking foolish risked diverting him away from his true mission as shepherd of the people.

The Socially Controlled

Not all shame-bound leaders are socially anxious. Some are the opposite—socialites who are eloquent and present themselves almost too well. These leaders seem to be incredibly poised but only maintain this by rigid social control of themselves and the environment around them. They avoid conflict or threatening situations, or go in all guns blazing. When they are threatened, they tend to become deeply defensive or project their own shame onto others.

Socially controlled leaders are typically very poor genuine collaborators and surround themselves with people who would never dare to disagree or challenge them. They often lever social constructs like honour and respect or even biblical instruction as means of ensuring that they remain unchallenged.

Social anxiety and social control are perhaps best seen as bookends between which most people fall. The key issue here is not identifying as either one, but identifying which elements in either behaviour we can relate to the most.

Deeper Shame

Beneath the visible symptoms of either social anxiety or social control lies the tree trunk of shame and the roots of where it came from. When psychologists Rick Hanson and Rick Mendius spoke to people with chronic shame, they found they used quite enduring words to describe their feelings, such as inadequacy, humiliation, guilt, remorse, embarrassment, and self-loathing.[5] These stable and unfortunately sharp and pervasive feelings form the trunk of the tree—one that has grown up over many years.[6]

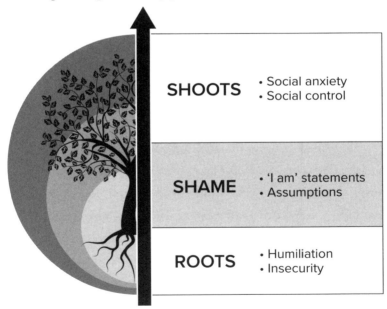

Figure 9: The roots and shoots of shame.

Several psychotherapists have come up with theories that try to explain where this kind of shame comes from, and not surprisingly, they've determined that shame has its roots in our pasts.[7] This is not to say that everyone who struggles with shame will have had a troubled past; instead, it comes from a complex matrix of experiences, dispositional factors, and reinforced learning. These theories tend to have two key components—past shaming experiences and early psychological development—which act together on whatever predisposition we may have.

We all relate to humiliating childhood experiences like wetting oneself in the middle of the school playground. These are often recalled by adults who are trying to make sense of their shame. Usually, a one-off event is not enough to start long-lasting shame. However, depending on the person's internal world, such an event may be a powerful trigger. It's not so much the individual humiliations or social mistakes that lead to shame, but rather the meaning we give to them. We assume that we may have been rejected or are about to be rejected—this is more important than the actual facts![8]

The way we perceive things and the assumptions we make about ourselves are rooted in deeper levels of our being. A healthy and nurturing childhood results in steady psychological development. For example, hungry, demanding babies later become young children who can be told to wait for mealtime, who in turn grow into older children who can recognise hunger and find food for themselves. Similar developments should occur in other areas of life, like how we form relationships.

However, when we perceive relationships to be threatening, or we fear being left out, our psychological development can become stuck. Shame causes us to seal over the growing roots of self-confidence to minimise damage.[9] We avoid the risk of further humiliation and instead become protective and avoidant. The root word of *shame* in Old English is *scamu*, meaning 'to cover'.[10] This is not a healthy covering of clothing for warmth, though; it is a negative covering over our inner pain because we don't know how to control it.[11] It's like bolting the basement door closed because we don't want the flood to 'get any worse'.

In chapter 1, we identified some of Moses' childhood challenges: He was (in his eyes) abandoned by his mother when she casted him adrift on the river in a basket. He was found among the bulrushes by a princess from another culture and raised as a prince. Later, as he struggled to understand his ethnicity, he killed an Egyptian whom he saw beating an Israelite slave.

He was terrified by the fact that he was able to kill someone, and also by how this was perceived: 'What I did must have become known.'[12] He exiled himself to Midian (his third culture) and, for forty years, took on the identity of a simple Midianite shepherd, which gave him the excuse to spend much time hidden away in the surrounding wilderness.

If we spend many years living with shame, we can form unhelpful 'I am' statements (sometimes called core beliefs). These 'statements' become hardwired and all too easily called upon. Here are a few examples:[13]

- I am defective (damaged, broken, a mistake, flawed)
- I am dirty (soiled, ugly, unclean, impure, filthy, disgusting)

- I am incompetent (not good enough, inept, ineffectual, useless)
- I am unwanted (unloved, unappreciated, uncherished)
- I am weak (small, impotent, puny, feeble)
- I am bad (awful, dreadful, evil, despicable)
- I am nothing (worthless, invisible, unnoticed, empty)

In Exodus 3:11, Moses asked, 'Who am I that I should go to Pharaoh and bring the Israelites out of Egypt?' After forty years of being a shepherd and having his head filled with statements like this, he did not feel worthy of the leadership God had for him. The shame that began as a surface issue, related to his immediate environment, became deeply established in the core of his being. Now, forty years later a great distance away from Egypt, Moses carried the same shame just as keenly.

Ants' nests regularly extend more than ten feet below ground, and a colony may contain several thousand ants. When a frustrated homeowner dusts the surface of the nest with ant powder, there is little initial impact. Yet with every ant's trip to the surface, the threat to the colony increases. The dust that was so far from the centre of the colony is inadvertently transported to its heart, and despite the nest remaining intact, all the life in it dies.

Carl Jung called shame 'a soul eating emotion'.[14] Just like the dusting of the ant powder, being shamed once is an experience that has little initial impact. Yet, as shaming experiences are repeated and carried into our hearts, they corrode our sense of identity and security. The impact is that we retreat from the emotional 'surface' of life and use a variety of mechanisms (which we are going to call 'shame skills') to function without the risk of further suffering.

SHAME STORIES

We all carry our own 'shame stories' made up of the two levels of shame we have just covered—the shoots and the roots. Have you noticed aspects of your own story as you have read this chapter so far? We may never understand fully why we have developed a particular shame story, but we can be sure that, left unaddressed, it will impact how we lead as well as our relationships with others.

Edward was a senior partner in a property lettings company. He was responsible for the management team and was also key to establishing new business, something that was essential to success in an industry with high turnover. On the surface, Edward appeared to be both a competent business leader and an effective manager; however, things were not as they seemed.

Whilst Edward kept the business stable, he was highly risk averse and overlooked many great business opportunities for the sake of stability. Within middle management there were two sorts of people: those who agreed with Edward and those who left. When his wife threatened to leave him, Edward had something of an emotional collapse. He couldn't understand why things were going wrong and why he had been labelled as 'controlling'.

Working with a leadership coach, Edward reflected upon his early experiences of rejection and abandonment during his parents' divorce and being sent to boarding school. He conceded that he was terrified of risk because of the high chance of failure. Ultimately, Edward worried that the shame he felt about himself would be revealed to the people around him and that they would reject and abandon him. Unfortunately, his attempts at damage limitation affected both his ability to lead and his relationships. Only dealing with his shame would bring a change to his circumstances.

Shame stories start early in life and can take a lot of unpicking. Even though I (Will) have wonderful and loving parents, the fact that I have wrestled with shame is proof that this emotion isn't exclusive to those from troubled families. Some people will have suffered humiliations, others have had times of insecurity, others have experienced more obvious emotional neglect and abuse. There is no simple diagnostic tool or need to join up all the dots—the human brain is a complex thing.

(Will): My first conscious memory of shame comes from my preschool years. I think I must have been ill and was left in the home whilst my mother dropped my sister at a neighbour's house for her journey to school. My memories of this absence are very powerful. What may have been a ten-minute trip seemed to last for an age in my young mind. I curled up on the floor in the hallway and prayed fervent prayers that mummy might come home. I can remember burying my face in Ted (my soft toy) in a state of deep distress that later vanished the moment I heard her key in the lock.

For reasons I do not understand, this early fear of abandonment became a central part of my shame story. This fear was quite unconscious until I experienced some really aggressive school bullying as an eleven-year-old.

I know that from that point onwards I began to associate anyone's separation from me with rejection. I'd believe that difficult experiences were my fault, rather than occurring as a benign reality of life. As shame quickly became a reinforcing spiral, normal moments of separation misinformed a view that I deserved to be left behind. Shame distorted my 'aloneness' into something that was malign and set me on a path to strive to be likeable. It drove me away from conflict and into appeasing others. Shame also tended to inhibit any leadership decisions I made that might be unpopular or controversial.

Most people have a shame story that remains buried. After Moses killed the Egyptian slave driver in Exodus 2:12, he 'hid him in the sand.' This act of burying ensured that Moses' shame story would dominate and influence his inner world until, and including, his exile from Egypt. Because he would not deliberately address it,[15] he would have little or no reprieve from its impact.

SHAME SKILLS

Not only is shame infinitely painful to experience, it also secures its own future. We feel shame—and then we feel shame about feeling shame. Leaders, as people who have a specific role to fulfil, cannot hide away, and so we develop 'shame skills': expert and intuitive responses to avoid further potentially shaming experiences. Just like the avoidance of social situations by the socially anxious, shame skills insulate us from our shame and keep us from ever testing the reality of our shame stories. Shame skills appear to offer us protection from further shaming experiences, when in fact they seal shame within and cause us to avoid circumstances that might provoke shame awareness.

In this way, it is possible to live your whole life defending against your own healing journey, like a man with a toothache who desperately avoids the dentist. We also deprive those around us of our real selves by pretending to be superhuman in ways that cannot be achieved authentically.

(Will): In 2005 when I had an anxiety breakdown following the London bombings, a dear friend and colleague came to see me and we took a walk together. It was the first time we had seen each other since I had been signed off work. When we began to talk about what I was going through, he turned to me and said, 'I am so relieved this has happened.' I felt immediately wounded. He continued, 'I had thought there was something wrong with me. I just couldn't match your capacity; it was like working with Superman and it just left me feeling very ordinary.' My shame and anxiety were not only driving me to break down, they were damaging my friends and colleagues as well.

Brennan Manning captured both of these aspects when he said, 'In a futile attempt to erase our past, we deprive the community of our healing gift. If we conceal our wounds out of fear and shame, our inner darkness can neither be illuminated nor become a light for others.'[16]

Sarah had a remarkable rejection story. She had been abandoned in childhood many times by the people who were responsible for her care. She became a Christian, and whilst she could articulate that story to illustrate the joy she felt about the faithfulness of God, her shame story was left unaddressed. Her 'powerful testimony' became a mechanism (shame skill) that she used to avoid addressing her early rejection.

The result of her early shame was a palpable distrust of the leaders around her and latterly the employees in her care. Because her shame story reinforced the belief that she was 'worthy of rejection', she became hypervigilant of potential rejections. Her shame skills also included: getting ahead of anyone who might reject her by rejecting them first, intense anger and emotionalism in the face of criticism, and moving on to new (less risky) relationships prematurely, where the pattern was repeated.

WHAT AM I TRYING TO DO WITH MY SHAME?

Many Christian talks, songs, and prayers offer 'freedom from emotions', as if our emotions should simply be turned off. This 'freedom' narrative generally suggests that only a small number of positive emotions are truly acceptable for Christians and an even smaller number are acceptable for leaders. 'No fear in life' sounds like a great motif, but it leads to a relatively rapid death as we dance in the middle of a motorway or swim in a crocodile-infested river!

Emotions, just like our physical bodies, are a fundamental, God-given part of our lives. But what began healthily can become unhealthy. If we become unwell in a part of our body, we don't remove it; we try to have it restored so it can be helpful and functional again. 'Functional' does not mean easy or positive, but functioning appropriately. Jesus expressed anger in Matthew 21:12, distress in Luke 12:50, grief in John 11:35, sorrow in Matthew 26:37, and despair in Mark 14:33. None of these emotions are easy or positive, but they are all appropriate in their context.

Far from being a benign reaction to humiliating circumstances, shame has the power to cover up our hurts and stifle our emotions. Shame can be the reason we get out of bed in the morning, and it can be the reason why we don't. Addressing the issue of shame is about enabling our emotions to be expressed in the appropriate contexts without the fear of rejection. Dealing with shame is about opening that locked door and bringing out the big pumps to drain the basement. Only when our foundations are exposed can we clear out the junk and set up the integrity gym!

STUDY GUIDE: CHAPTER 3

Can you think of instances in your life when something that was meant for your good turned into a shaming experience? List any you are comfortable writing down.

Are you socially anxious, and do you avoid difficult situations? Or are you social controlling and make sure things happen your way?

Are you able to describe your 'shame story'? Try to include any early memories, feelings, and themes that come to you.

What 'shame skills' have you developed because of your shame story? Try and list the key ones below.

Chapter 4

HOW TO PICK UP A SNAKE

'The secret to happiness is freedom, and
the key to freedom is courage'.[1]
Thucydides

We introduced Moses' state of shame in the previous chapters—both his social anxiety and his deep sense of personal unworthiness in fulfilling God's calling on his life. Picking up the story that God revealed to me (Will) on my retreat in the mountains of North Carolina, we read:

> The LORD said to him, 'What is that in your hand?' 'A staff,' he replied. The LORD said, 'Throw it on the ground.' Moses threw it on the ground and it became a snake, and he ran from it. Then the LORD said to him, 'Reach out your hand and take it by the tail.' So Moses reached out and took hold of the snake and it turned back into a staff in his hand.[2]

Having read this passage many times before, its significance was initially unclear. But as I reflected on this biblical text, I addressed the question to myself: 'Will, how would *you* pick up a snake?'

The truth is, I dislike snakes and I wouldn't pick it up at all. In fact, I would run from it as Moses did. But, if I had to pick it up, it wouldn't be by the tail. Any animal picked up by the tail is likely to bite you, and a snake carries the risks of having both sharp fangs and powerful venom.

With only a basic knowledge of snakes, we would all likely struggle with God's instruction; but to a shepherd in the fourteenth century BC, this would have been an actual life-or-death decision. Moses had spent forty years protecting his flocks from the dangers of desert snakes, and to bend down and pick up this snake by the tail would have been the most counterintuitive decision of his life.

That is when I began to see God's question as a revelation about the way in which I was responding to shame in my own life. I was an expert at running from it, and I was equally accomplished at looking good on the outside but feeling bad on the inside. What I had absolutely no intention of doing was picking up my shame in case it bit me and I died of humiliation.

THE SHAME BREAK

Typically, our first response to shame is to run away and hope that we can shake off the risks of un-belonging. Many of us avoid places or people which evoke a shame memory within us. People commonly talk about making a 'clean break' when they are really making a 'shame break'.

The trouble with a 'shame break' is that there is never any resolution—just avoidance. The place or places that provoke our shame become off limits to us. For Moses, the desert had become his 'shame break', and Egypt was off limits to him. The lack of belonging he felt on the day he left was still as real to him forty years later. Of course, his shame wasn't actually located in Egypt; it was in him, which was why running away from it was so counterproductive.

> (Rob): I often have conversations with patients who are thinking about moving to another town. They want to know if their problems will be better if they move away from their current stressors, which often include family. My usual response is that when they move to a new town, their head moves with them. Family may be physically more distant from them, but their internal representations of family will travel with them too. The reality is that you cannot leave how you really feel behind in another location.

CONTROLLING THE SHAME SNAKE

When shame isn't related to a physical place but instead to a period of time, such as our adolescence, making a 'shame break' becomes even more difficult. We can't run from the snake, so we hold it tightly, controlling it to ensure that we never get bitten.

Controlling shame is a complex process, and people use all sorts of mechanisms to achieve it. Some will reinvent themselves through fashion, exercise, education, or a new persona—cutting off their old life entirely. Others will use subtle but equally determined measures to make sure that nobody can ever get beneath their armour and see their real vulnerabilities.

> (Will): When I went up to Cambridge as an under-graduate, I contacted an old friend from school who was a year ahead of me. When we met, he was with some of his new friends and I was amazed. My friend's accent had become very smart, he had exchanged hoodies for tweed jackets and trainers for velvet slippers. There was literally nothing about him that I recognised. The setting was too public for me to react openly, so I played along. I tried to ask a few questions relating back to the old days at home, but I could sense his terror that I might expose the facade to his friends. Instead I didn't press further, and we didn't really see each other after that.

Being on the receiving end of situations like this can make us feel angry and frustrated. Has our friend forgotten their roots and was our old friendship not good enough? We take it personally, but the person likely just feels vulnerable and anxious about being humiliated. I (Will) later discovered that my friend had a lot of shame and embarrassment about a family situation back at home. This metamorphosis was his attempt to cut himself off from the shame and reinvent himself in a way that ensured that he belonged to the new group.

A great danger of running from or controlling shame is how good it feels. When we escape the emotion of shame, we feel deep relief. Our disgust and humiliation are kept at bay, and we can feel safe in the knowledge that we belong somewhere new—except for the fact that the escape is not real. Like skating across a pond which is only covered by thin ice, we can glide along just fine until we take a tumble and fall right through.

Moses spent forty years living with the Midianites; he married a Midianite, he was mentored by a Midianite, he looked after Midianite sheep, but at no point in his story did Moses ever believe he *was* a Midianite. In the same way, when shame says, 'You don't belong here,' no amount of assimilation and success will make you feel that you really belong.

(Will): I was once invited to a dinner party by a dear friend who is now a successful film director but was a rising star at the time. I recognised some 'faces' from television, but they had no idea who I was and seemed to assume I was a rising star too. I listened politely to their ideas—which seemed to encourage them.

Finally, during pudding, the television presenter on my left asked me directly, 'So what exactly do you do?' I replied, 'Oh, I'm not in the media. I am a teacher.' At that point, she gave me a look that would have sunk a thousand ships and moved around to the other side of the table. I was left silently eating my pudding with a very obvious gap next to me which spoke loudly, 'You don't belong here.'

Figure 10: Will trying not to look like an important media person.

FEELING LIKE A FRAUD

Shame-bound leaders are plagued by the fear of being found out—it is one of the greatest inhibitors to their leadership. On one level they know that they are overestimating the threat of rejection, but just like controlling the snake, it feels safer to overestimate its venom than to underestimate it.

Leadership feels like a trap where you know it would be better to be authentic, but equally, if people knew your mistakes, thoughts, weaknesses, and vulnerabilities, then they would reject and humiliate you anyway. The most natural thing to do is just run away from the snake and back to the desert of Midian!

PROFESSIONAL TO PERSONAL ESTEEM

We have worked with leaders in a wide spectrum of fields—medical, sporting, academic, religious, business—and have met many successful and seemingly confident people who struggle with low self-esteem. They are unable to transfer their 'professional self-esteem' (for example, knowing that you are a fast runner or good strategist) into a genuine feeling that 'I belong here'.

It can almost seem that the more successful people are in their chosen areas, the more they feel like frauds. The disparity between what people believe about them and what they believe about themselves becomes an increasingly wide chasm, which makes them feel even less comfortable in their leadership role.

Sigmund Freud said, 'That which we can't remember, we will repeat,' meaning that unless we spend some time remembering and working through our shame, we will repeat the same old mistakes and keep on feeling like frauds. In his classic paper 'Remembering, Repeating and Working Through',[3] Freud explained how this suppression needs to be brought out into the open, not run away from or controlled. There will be unconscious resistance to this, but if done within supportive relationships, the person can undergo great healing. Brené Brown said, 'Shame cannot survive being spoken. It cannot survive empathy.'[4] If empathy and acceptance can replace fear and distrust, then progress can be made—which is why it is so important for leaders to have real 'belonging-based' relationships.

In our work at the Mind and Soul Foundation, we have come across countless leaders who feel both trapped and fraudulent. Common refrains are:

- If people knew the real me, they would never respect me, let alone follow me

- I never share how I feel because I know people hate weakness
- I don't deserve to be where I am
- I let people think they know me, but I am only 'real' at home
- I feel lonely most of the time—people are with me, but they don't know me
- Who people think I am and who I feel I am is increasingly disconnected

They experience ambient shame in most settings and yo-yo between trying to control the narrative and wanting to just run away. Like Moses they are staring at the snake of shame and locked by indecision, fearing potential humiliation but also feeling frustrated by their fettered leadership. Leaders, for the most part, can't run away, and so they hide in plain sight. They can be casting a company vision on collaboration yet share their plans with no one. They can preach a sermon on the church as a community, yet the mask remains in place. They can talk about being open and authentic yet manage to share nothing of any note.

GRASPING THE SNAKE'S TAIL

Why might God have instructed Moses to pick up the snake by the tail? Here was a highly defensive leader whose staff was a symbol of his 'small power' in the desert of Midian. If God was going to enable Moses to begin his true mission as shepherd of Israel and exercise 'big power', He needed to deal with Moses' shame story.

The snake was a recognised symbol of Egypt[5] and represented the shame Moses had left behind: it was a sign of all that Moses had run from—the fear, the guilt, the humiliation. God's challenge to Moses was one of huge significance. He effectively asked Moses three life-changing questions:

1. Are you willing to act against your defensiveness and in obedience to My will? (Obedience)

2. Are you willing to risk the potential of being bitten by the snake for the sake of a life of true leadership? (Instinct)

3. Are you willing to accept that My unique provision for your leadership is perfect? (Provision)

Moses' journey from having the staff of a shepherd to having the staff of a true leader required picking up the snake by the tail. It was a sign of his agreement with all that God was asking of him. It was the moment when he flipped from running away to running towards. It was the moment when he first carried the authority of God in his leadership. The preaching notes for this passage written by eighteenth-century preacher John Wesley suggest that God called Moses to carry the staff, 'that he might not be ashamed of that mean condition out of which God called him [a shepherd]. This rod must be his staff of authority.'[6]

Figure 11: The essential journey Moses had to make—from shepherd to leader.

Wesley identified shame and authority as the battling elements of effective leadership. He constantly referred back to Scripture to undo his shame and reassert his authority in Christ: 'This would furnish us with matter of praise, where we found God had enabled us to conform to his blessed will, and matter of humiliation and prayer, where we were conscious of having fallen short.'[7] To find mastery over shame is to be released not only to greater authority in leadership but also to authenticity of leadership. Moses had run away and created a new 'lesser mission' for himself, but in reaching for the snake's tail, his shame was undone and his authority to lead was restored. He was on his way to fulfil his true mission with 'big power'. For the first time in his life, Moses knew that he belonged.

THREE KEY DECISIONS

Overcoming shame in our own leadership follows a similar course to Moses', although there are no tangible snakes to pick up! Our reluctance to change, however, will be no less powerful.

Moses had to throw down what little power he had to find a greater power. Most shame-bound leaders want to hold on to their shepherd staffs because they feel unworthy of anything greater. They are also terrified of losing anything that validates their leadership and of letting go of any small bit of power they have.

Moses had to pick up his shame snake by the tail. That was an exercise in owning his story and facing the reality that shame bites! He would have to endure the venom of Pharaoh and even some venom from the Israelites. And they would all be asking him every question that he had been trying to escape from: 'Who do you think you are?' 'Do you really belong here?' 'Did God really send you?'

Shame-bound leaders are risk averse and highly defensive. Exposing ourselves to the risk of humiliation, exposure, and unbelonging is completely counterintuitive, and yet it is the only way to hold the staff of God's true mission for our lives.

The Decision for Obedience

It is God who calls and justifies our leadership. Our human estimation—or the enemy's accusations—keeps us from an act of simple obedience to God. King David wrote in Psalm 25:2, 'I trust in you; do not let me be put to shame, nor let my enemies triumph over me.' Much of overcoming shame is found in the simple act of obeying God, accepting that we belong here despite the condemnation of our own hearts.

We can often do nothing better than simply to say, 'God, You have called me to this; Your judgement is perfect and I choose to be obedient to Your call.' The exact nature of this decision will be different for each leader and is not restricted to church roles. God calls us in many areas of life—and has equipped us all for His call.

The Decision *against* Instinct

Approaching shame in a new way is entirely counter-instinctual— Moses didn't need to be told to run from the snake. Many people's leadership is thwarted by the power of their instinctual responses. They say, 'I just felt I had to …'—feeling absolutely compelled to act in a repetitive, instinctual way, which is what forms a habit. This is why making a decision against instinct is a foundation stone on the journey to true belonging. If we keep defending ourselves against shame with the same hardwired mechanisms, nothing will ever change. We will just repeat our same defensive patterns of leading. Wearing a life jacket is not swimming; it's floating! Ultimately the decision to make ourselves vulnerable to the rejection of others (drowning) is also the moment at which we can belong with others (start really swimming). Moses was done with running. Are you?

The Decision *for* Provision

When Moses made himself vulnerable to the snake's bite, the snake of his shame turned into his staff of authority. It was at this moment in Moses' leadership that he moved from outsider to insider, his shame was undone, his calling was revealed, and God's provision was placed in his hands. When we accept the provision of God, we demonstrate our authority as His children and the power of an innate belonging that nothing can overcome.

(Rob): I had finished my foundation year after qualifying as a doctor. I'd moved from Cambridge, where I was at university, to Leeds, where I had got involved in the student ministry at my church. I wanted to do psychiatry, so I applied for psychiatry training schemes. The day before the interviews were scheduled to start in Leeds, I had yet to hear anything, so I phoned up to enquire. In my pride, I assumed my application had been mistakenly overlooked—instead they told me I had not been shortlisted. I was floored.

I was tempted to run (I'd also applied to the scheme in the very north of Scotland) or to try and control things (I'd applied back to Cambridge too), but I knew deep down that God wanted me in Leeds. So, the day after my initial phone call, I did the risky thing and phoned up all the other locations outside Leeds that I had applied to, and withdrew my applications.

The day after that I received a call from the Leeds office to say that they still had one unfilled post and asked if I would attend an interview: I got that place!

MAKING IT REAL

The act of making these three key decisions is surprisingly hard, not least because the situations in which we need to make them will be naturally uncomfortable. When shame and humiliation are threatening us, the compelling powers of instinct and self-preservation kick in. Yet it is at these precise times when we can also begin to make new and powerful stands around trust, obedience, and belonging. Rev. Stephen Foster said, 'I have regretted many of the decisions I have made in my life, but I have never once regretted an act of obedience to Jesus Christ.'[8]

The greatest opportunities we have to 'pick up the snake' may well be times when we have done something wrong, like Moses who hadn't equated a burning bush with it being holy ground.[9] We can all recall times when we have had to take responsibility for mistakes we have made, but vulnerability and authenticity rarely result in the humiliation and rejection that we anticipate.

> (Rob): I was a trainee psychiatrist and made a poor decision one night when on call—giving medication to someone who was seeking drugs. I was summoned to a 7:30 a.m. meeting with the unit's boss, who was one of the UK's most senior psychiatrists. I admitted my mistake and asked him to explain how to get this right next time around. He appreciated my vulnerability and we got on very well thereafter. He even gave me a job reference.

(Will): I was new to a role and made a hasty phone call that resulted in some hurt and embarrassment to others. At the debrief with one of the senior team, I was tempted to act defensively. But instead, I was vulnerable about how anxious I had felt at the time and I apologised deeply for the pain I had caused. It was a very hard conversation but ultimately a good one: the senior leader is now my mentor and a very dear friend.

In these examples, we unlocked the shame basement and let in some light. The facade of the omnicompetent psychiatrist/pastor who always made good decisions had cracked, and our real selves showed up in those meetings. We went in feeling that we had to make everything right but walked out knowing that we could make mistakes and still belong. We were even offered guidance, direction, and support.

CROSSING OVER

These moments of making key decisions may happen only a handful of times each year, but they are key reference points on our journey to belonging. Moses' encounter with the snake was a line in the sand: it was an opportunity to either turn away from freedom or turn towards it. Choosing real freedom is costly and often frightening, but it is still a choice.

Figure 12: Ready to set out on a new adventure in leadership?

At this midway point on our journey, are you ready to cross over? If so, it will require you prayerfully accepting that …

- Shame is inhibiting my leadership and undermining my sense of true belonging
- My emotions are not always reliable because shame distorts them to exaggerate the risk of rejection
- My decisions are often distorted to instinctually protect me from exposure or humiliation
- 'Picking up the snake' is a choice to live more vulnerably, accepting the risk of rejection (being bitten)
- God wants to establish my leadership in a belonging-based relationship with Him
- God offers me a greater authority once I have laid down my attempts to justify my own leadership
- Crossing over is not a one-off decision but an attitude of my heart to obedience, vulnerability, and trust

STUDY GUIDE: CHAPTER 4

How have you been tempted to run away from or control shameful situations?

Are you afraid of being found out? Do you identify with the idea that you might be a fraud? If so, how?

Which of the three decisions (for obedience, against instinct, for provision) seems the hardest to you? Why?

Are you ready to cross over? If you are not sure, what is holding you back?

Chapter 5

SECURITY AND SUCCESS

'It's insecurity that is always chasing you and
standing in the way of your dreams.'[1]
Vin Diesel

A common leadership myth says that success is the route to security. Leaders say things like, 'Just one more big deal and I will be secure.' 'Just one more promotion and I will be set for the future.' The fact is that success rarely leads to security; very often it does the opposite. We believe that having inner security provides the context from which you are far more likely to achieve success.

Jesus teaches us about two builders in Matthew 7:24–27. One began with security and found success, and the other began with success and found insecurity. Verse 25 describes three challenges to the house's security: 'The rain came down, the streams rose, and the winds blew.' These are like the challenges of leadership: the rain of unfavourable circumstances will impact your leadership; you cannot predict it, and you certainly cannot stop it. These circumstances negatively impact the things that are under your leadership and soon you are standing ankle deep in problems. Then the wind of opposition—criticism, disloyalty, division, and disunity—begins to blow, and it isn't long before it is beating on your house. Both houses experience the same challenges, but their foundations determine whether they stand or fall.

> (Will): A few years ago I was returning from taking my children to school when I walked past a pretty old house that stands alongside the River Thames. Rob knows the house too, from his years rowing! It had belonged to a famous pop star, but she recently sold it to a mobile phone magnate.
>
> The new owner decided to build a giant basement under the house, which was an interesting decision given that it is situated fewer than ten metres from one of Europe's biggest rivers. The builders clearly hadn't secured the foundations properly and the sandy riverside soil began to give way under the weight of the building above. On the morning that I was walking by, the house had become critically destabilised, and I watched as the entire property collapsed onto the ground. Miraculously, no one was hurt.

Belonging-based leadership is more than just dealing with shame that has held you back in the past. It is also about paying close attention to your remaining foundations, particularly to weak spots that are likely to cause issues in the future. If our foundations are weak, the storms of leadership will quickly provoke us to use the same old shame-based strategies for survival. That flooded church basement needed more than just being pumped out. It needed regular basement inspections, brickwork repairs, and even the installation of an automatic pump to deal with any potential future floods.

FAULTY FIXES

Addressing issues with our emotional foundations takes both awareness and courage; there are no shortcuts. We meet leaders who, despite knowing that they are vulnerable, try to avoid addressing their foundations at all costs. This attitude is akin to finding the flood and simply relocking the basement in the vain hope that it will fix itself. They say things like:

'If you give these things too much attention, they will take you over.'

'I have prayed it through, and I know that God has it in His hands.'

'If you start talking about this sort of problem, it's a slippery slope towards a breakdown!'

'I just need to get on with my calling and not get distracted by emotional stuff.'

'This all seems a bit self-absorbed. I haven't got time for this.'

Sigmund Freud's daughter, Anna, first described these 'defence mechanisms' in 1936.[2] Just like the basement door, they are the mechanisms that we develop to keep other people away from our emotional world: overworking/hyper-busyness, over-spiritualising, irritability/hostility, dismissiveness. Becoming highly defensive keeps us disconnected from ourselves and others and unable to address the problems that we carry. Emotional defences usually sound reasonable (even virtuous), but they are just a diversion to protect the status quo. This is the issue of leader insecurity.

'Insecurity' is ironic, in that the people with the most heightened defences are invariably the most insecure; they are usually also the most isolated. Abraham Maslow described an insecure person as one who 'perceives the world as a threatening jungle and most human beings as dangerous and selfish.'[3] The sense of emotional threat amongst Christian leaders is very high, and they are particularly vulnerable to becoming defensive. This is partly because they rarely believe that they meet the expected standard and also because of the real threat of the judgement of others, not to mention the pressure of thinking they need to perform perfectly. Pastor Bill Johnson said, 'If you don't live by the praises of men then you won't die by their criticisms.'[4]

SELF-COMPASSION

Once you have become aware of your defence mechanisms it is easy to become frustrated by them and self-critical. Leaders are particularly prone to a harsh 'inner critic' that attacks them from the first moment they realise that they may have been working counter-productively. It is important that you don't bully yourself. The reality is that we all use defences of one kind or another. They are developed over a long period of time and often under great pressure.

Christian leaders are just as likely to become defensive as anyone else: gossip around integrity, disparaging remarks about their talk delivery or people management, even questions about spiritual fervour or biblical interpretation are a reality for many. Recognising that 'bolting the basement door' is a natural (not a stupid) reaction is a critical step towards belonging. Defences that keep us from being vulnerable are problematic, and making positive change is only possible when we feel safe, and that includes with ourselves.

> Moses cited his stutter as a reason for not being up to the task at hand. However, in Exodus 6:30, it was apparent that his real concern was not his stutter but his belief that Pharaoh would not listen to him. Like many shame-bound leaders, Moses was fearful of humiliation, he was insecure about his competences, and he had a tendency towards hiding.
>
> In a demonstration of grace, God's anger briefly burned against Moses, but He allowed his brother Aaron (at the age of eighty-three) to speak for Him. God was not going to let anything stand in the way of Moses fulfilling his true mission: to set the Israelites free.

THE HIDING DEFENCE

Hiding was Moses' most instinctual defence. He had spent forty years hiding in the Midian desert, and despite having 'picked up the snake', he had not completely overcome his old habit. That is why 'draining the shame basement' isn't enough on its own; we have to address our foundations and put new behaviours into practice.

Moses had made dramatic progress, but he still ended up hiding behind Aaron as his spokesperson. He was technically still the leader, but he had a projection of himself to hide behind. For Moses, this was a physical projection, but for most of us today, it is an emotional projection—the bit of ourselves we are happy to show; a 'false self' to hide behind, even to lead from behind.

In this digital age we have the tools to create convincing and powerful public profiles, and we can manage our social media identities to the finest detail. We can script our lives for public consumption, whilst living in a completely different reality. Leaders are often celebrated on social media as being 'so vulnerable' when their vulnerability has been contrived to provoke that precise reaction.

In a radically connected world you would think that there would be greater community, but leaders are telling us that they have never felt so lonely. One study in the *American Journal of Preventive Medicine* concluded that those in 'high social media user groups' were three times more likely to have increased 'Perceived Social Isolation' when compared to lower-use groups.[5] In an age of connectedness, it is belongingness that we need.

Theologian and mystic Thomas Merton wrote, 'Every one of us is shadowed by an illusory person: a False Self. My false and private self is the one who wants to exist outside the reach of God's will and God's love … outside of reality and outside of life. And such a self cannot help but be an illusion.'[6] Merton knew the motivation but did not live to see the means or ease with which today's leaders could lever their false selves and lead from the shadows.

BUILDING A FALSE SELF

A false self is not just a benign screen to hide behind; it is a complex and purposeful representation of ourselves. A bit like a social media profile, a false self is carefully crafted to carry the aspirations, if not the realities, of a persons' life. This idealised self-image presents the parts of ourselves which we are most proud of, those which we deem to be most acceptable or profitable and so (we think) will offer the best gateway to belonging. Unconsciously at least, we create a false self because we believe that people will like it far more than they will like us.

Our false self stands opposed to our shame state which, whilst containing true parts of ourselves, is also a distortion of who we really are. Our true selves are sandwiched between who we hope we are not and who we hope others will think we are. You can see how the more we believe in our shame state, the more likely we are to create a powerful false self. Shame makes us believe that we won't belong, and that provokes us to create a defence which ensures that we cannot belong.

Figure 13: Shame state (basement) – true self (reality) – false self (shop window).

The false self provides the means for us to hide in plain sight by projecting such an attractive and useful version of ourselves that others are too distracted to catch sight of the shame state (who we fear we may be). We can increase our apparent usefulness or 'fit' by adapting our false self to fill a vacant role in an organisation or social group. We may become the joker, the carer, the wise sage, the dependable or needy child.

Our false self (idealised *ego image*) is built around the premise that we have positive attributes to trade for people's affections and loyalties. It is not that we can choose to be exactly who we want, but we can finesse what we have in a way that makes us look more attractive or acceptable—whilst keeping our shame basement securely locked and out of sight. Window dressing for the soul.

SAFETY NET OR POACHER'S TRAP?

The false self can feel like a safety net that keeps us away from the dangers of rejection and humiliation, but it is far more like a poacher's trap. In the words of the poet Sir Walter Scott, 'What a tangled web we weave when we first practice to deceive.'[7] If we become tangled up in a false self, we are safe from feeling true rejection, but we are also blocked from experiencing true belonging.

Our sense of impending rejection never allows us to rest. Like someone keeping a big secret, we have to work really hard to keep the shop window sparkling and attractive. The false self requires us to keep relationships mobile and shallow, a bit like a stream where the water rushes over the boulders and stones. So long as things are moving, people tend to focus on the surface rather than what is underneath. Still waters, on the other hand, run deep, and you can look down as far as you wish into the depths below.

WEAKENING THE FALSE SELF

Despite being a powerful defence mechanism, the false self can be brought into our awareness and challenged. We can notice the instability of projecting the false self whilst keeping our shame basement locked. We can see the shallow victory of dodging criticism by showing only part of ourselves. We can acknowledge that we will never receive the genuine credit that people want to give us. We can accept the exhaustion and isolation that come from having to keep up appearances all the time.

Becoming self-aware can stop us from reacting in the same old ways. Instead it can help us to make healthy, conscious choices to reveal more of who we are authentically. These new ways of being can then actively foster our belonging by connecting with people through our vulnerabilities, accepting the compassion and help of others, receiving the belonging that is already being offered to us, and experiencing the relief of being known and accepted.

Good Parts of Our Character Get Buried

Not everything in the basement is bad! In fact, much of what constitutes our shame state is actually neutral or good. Our basement may be infused with shame, but it is also filled with our foibles and oddities. We connect with people through these vulnerabilities far more than we do our strengths, so hiding them away from others leaves us belonging *less*, not more.

We Appear to Need People Less

One important aspect of our belonging is built around altruism and compassion. We bury our needs as weak aspects of the self that don't fit with the confident false self that we have created. This prevents us from giving others a sense of purpose and value. If we reject their helping, they in turn feel powerless and ashamed and move away from us, for they feel they have nothing to offer us.

We Disregard Our Actual Belonging

One of the most heartbreaking aspects of the false self is how our true belonging is often disregarded. In acknowledging the split between shop window and shame basement, we tell ourselves that we aren't accepted because we aren't fully known. We assume that the genuine praise we receive is purely for the window dressing and would be withdrawn if the basement were revealed. Weakening the false self by experimenting with greater vulnerability can help us to realise that we are far more acceptable than we believe.

> Jerry was the son of a well-known Christian leader and radio broadcaster. Because his moments of childhood failure were the best illustrations for parenting anecdotes, his parents often featured his stories—like the time he ate dog food from the dog's bowl. Whenever he met a listener in real life, he felt he had to act the part to preserve his parents' reputation.

As time went on, Jerry developed a false self. His shop window was 'humble, teachable, redeemed Jerry'. He gave people what they wanted to hear—that teenagers can become lovely, reflective, well-adjusted individuals. Twenty years later, he was still the 'humble, teachable' guy from his parents' shows, but his shame basement was full to bursting with rage and frustration.

Buried in the basement were the gifts that Jerry had needed in his adult life and leadership—his decisiveness, his strategy, his honour. Yet to open the door on these things risked being rejected and losing the well-loved pastiche that he had constructed over decades.

SHADOW MISSIONS

Sustaining a false self requires a lot of effort and leaves us with unmet emotional needs. Consequently, most defensive leaders develop strategies that both support their false self and give them the emotional rewards they crave. These are what psychologist and pastor John Ortberg calls our 'Shadow Missions'.[8]

Ortberg wrote, 'Leaders love to think about mission, love to strategize about mission, love to cast vision for mission, love to achieve mission, love to celebrate mission. And everybody has a shadow mission. Our lives and the lives of the groups we're part of can drift.'[9] You can dedicate your life to fulfilling your true mission and yet be running an unseen self-referencing parallel mission. Over time that shadow mission can subtly drift into the dominant position of your life.

Since our greatest unmet need is to belong authentically, shadow missions act to give us a 'belonging high' through the praise or affirmation of others, or they work towards self-justification through over-achievement or competition. And these subtle strategies are typically just 5 degrees away from the leader's true mission.

Figure 14: Our shadow missions are only 5 degrees off course.

Moses' true mission (explored in chapter 4) was to shepherd the lost sheep of Israel to the Promised Land. His shadow mission was just to shepherd sheep and protect his 'simple shepherd Hebrew' false self. By fulfilling all of the shadow roles below, he could stay in hiding, keeping his shame buried and never having to face the fear of being tested and found wanting.

Moses fled to Midian and fulfilled a number of shadow roles. He drew water from a well for some animals (Exodus 2:15, 17) rather than being the person who refreshed the enslaved Israelites in Egypt. He worked for a priest (verses 16, 21) rather than serving as the spiritual leader of the people himself. He became the eligible bachelor by rescuing the priest's daughters (verse 17), one of whom he then accepted as his wife (verse

> 21), and he fathered a son (verse 22) instead of a nation. In bitter irony, Moses named the child 'Gershom', saying, 'I have become a foreigner in a foreign land,' when all the evidence seemed to suggest that he was very much at home!

Leaders are fiercely defensive of their shadow missions, even convincing themselves that they are worthy enterprises. Ortberg said of the shadow mission, 'To face a difficult truth without getting discouraged or defensive is one of the great challenges of a leader.'[10] Our defensiveness is vastly disproportionate to the shadow mission, because it is not the activity that is at stake, but our entire idealised *ego image*. If we expose the activities that prop up our false self, it is just a short step towards the whole house crumbling to the ground.

EXPOSING THE SHADOW

Acknowledging and identifying your shadow mission is another aspect of 'picking up the snake'. Shadows tend not to respond well to the exposure of plentiful light. By gaining an awareness of the things we do to prop ourselves up, and with God's help, we can become able to make authentic, true mission-based decisions.

> Will's false self is an entertainer—always on form, self-depreciating, and telling funny stories. He hides his 'basement' of vulnerability, melancholy, and sense of uncertainty. He can use his shadow mission to 'make people like him' instead of fulfilling his true mission to preach the good news.

On a Sunday, he could preach two different sermons that have exactly the same content. Sermon A is about the faithfulness of God. Sermon B is about the wit of Will van der Hart. Sermon B sounds exactly the same as sermon A, but its intention is not to fulfil his mission for Christ; it is designed to fulfil his shadow mission for himself.

Rob's false self is a 'good' psychiatrist, maybe even one 'slightly better than average'. Well liked, avoiding difficult encounters with difficult patients who don't say nice things, preferring the 'rosy glow' of a consultation where everyone is pleased with the outcome.

However, just because everyone is pleased does not mean that the correct decisions have been made. Sometimes it is necessary to be disliked.

We hope that this book will be a trigger for the exploration of your own shadow mission. It could be that you will gain insight on your faulty strategies from trusted friends or a counsellor. This is not a smooth process, and even when you realise the need to change, the desire to default back to old strategies can be potent. Addressing the shadow mission can feel very threatening, but it is essential in the journey to greater belonging. As Jesus said in John 12:24, 'Unless a grain of wheat falls to the ground and dies, it remains only a single seed. But if it dies, it produces many seeds.'

Moses struggled to leave his shadow behind, as he led the people out of Israel and across the Red Sea. He had turned

> foul water into fresh, brought them manna and quail, but he was persistently independent and feared humiliation. They finally ended their time in 'the desert of sin' and approached Mount Sinai, but they were again without water.
>
> In Numbers 20:8, the Lord commands Moses, 'Speak to that rock before their eyes and it will pour out its water.'
>
> Instead, verse 11 shows us that Moses struck the rock with his staff. Could this have been his shadow mission at work again? Fearing humiliation in front of the elders?
>
> God says in verse 12, 'Because you did not trust in me enough to honour me as holy in the sight of the Israelites, you will not bring this community into the land I give them.'

By God's grace, we will not face the same literal consequences as Moses. Jesus has paid the price for our sin, and we *can* enter the Promised Land. But we need to live in the light of the revelation of His love and sufficiency. This means a decision to stop using our shadow missions to try to achieve a belonging that can only be found in true relationship with God and others. Ultimately, we need to allow our false selves to die if we are going to start living, let alone leading.

THE JOURNEY TO BELONGING

The journey to belonging we are talking about is found in many of the great myths and movies and is commonly called the 'Hero's Journey'.[11] We see it in the ancient Greek legend of Odysseus, Bible characters like Job and David, fairy tales like the Ugly Duckling or Cinderella, and movies like *Star Wars*. The basic principle is that you carry something (a leadership role), then you lose pretty much everything (the falling), and then you get it all back again (leadership again). However, this time it looks different—perhaps *feels* different is a better description.

Many of the Hero's Journey stories have a very dramatic episode of 'falling' that are typically external to them. Perhaps it is getting lost on a mountain, losing a battle, or enduring a life-changing injury like St. Ignatius (founder of the Society of Jesus) who was shot in the leg with a cannon ball!

For most people, the falling is a very quiet and internal experience. It could be an episode of depression or low mood, a struggle at work or in a relationship, or perhaps just a simple awareness that you have come to the end of your own resources.

There are a number of key stages to the journey that are worth looking out for. These are not things you can manufacture, but they can help you become aware of how your life is changing as you die to your false self and shadow missions and reconnect with the true mission God has called you to.

(Rob): I have been on such an adventure for two years. The 'supernatural aid' was a combination of a particularly dark Scottish winter and a number of prayers being answered at the same time. A friend recommended a book, which introduced me to the Hero's Journey—I was forty years old and I was at either a mid-life crisis or a mid-life change.

There were many deaths—friends who didn't keep in touch, leaving behind roles that gave self-esteem, missing Scotland. I was not in the driving seat—my usual place of control. However, after death came life. We decided this was a time-limited adventure and made plans to return to the UK. I have a renewed energy to work again for the NHS and the Mind and Soul Foundation. I expect my life will look much the same to the casual observer as it did before I left, but I know for me, it will feel radically different.

Figure 15: The Hero's Journey.

Signpost 1: A Call to Adventure

Have you caught a vision for a life of belonging? An adventure in which your leadership is an expression of your authentic self? One in which you can make mistakes and enjoy successes without fear? Have you felt a call to a greater freedom in which your life is uncoupled from the need to achieve for the sake of your public image?

Signpost 2: Supernatural Aid

Has something provoked your exploration of belonging? Perhaps it has been a series of barely perceptible challenges or maybe something much more dramatic like a back injury or a personal loss. Have you sensed God challenging you to explore your life with greater honesty?

Signpost 3: A Helper

Have you found people on this road who have been an encouragement to you? Have you asked others what you think your shadow mission might be? Whilst this is ultimately a personal journey that you must follow alone with God, there are people, and resources written by those who have gone this way before, that will guide you.[12]

Signpost 4: Death and Rebirth

'Are you tired? Worn out? Burned out on religion?'[13] Have you come to the end of yourself? The best-kept secret about falling is that it is freeing. After death comes life, after striving comes resting. Crises are rarely a crisis that we think they are. Now that things are understood at a deeper level, belonging-based leadership can start.

Signpost 5: The Return and Re-gifting

The shepherd's staff has now become the leader's staff. Picking up the snake by the tail looked like certain death, but it was actually the gateway to certain life. The insecure leader is now a secure one. How is your life being transformed and resourced by God? What might God be calling you to return to? How has the true mission of your life been renewed?

STUDY GUIDE: CHAPTER 5

When reflecting on your journey to belonging, which foundations do you think need to be strengthened in your emotional basement?

How would you describe your own false self? How do you hope that people will see you? List the attributes in order of importance to you:

1.
2.
3.
4.
5.

Can you identify your shadow mission? In which way does it help to reveal the attributes listed above?

How far along the Journey to Belonging do you find yourself? Comment on the following stages:

The call to adventure:

A supernatural aid:

A helper:

Death and rebirth:

Return and re-gifting:

Chapter 6

RELATIONALISM

'If a tree falls in the forest and no one
hears it, does it make a sound?'[1]

Rev. George Berkeley

George Berkeley answered his own philosophical question with a resounding 'Yes'. He believed God was everywhere and so God had heard the tree fall. The view that reality exists within the context of relationships is called relationalism.[2] But this is not just the preserve of philosophy; it is a biblical notion. Paul wrote in 1 Corinthians 2:14–16:

> The unspiritual self, just as it is by nature, can't receive the gifts of God's Spirit. There's no capacity for them. They seem like so much silliness. Spirit can be known only by spirit—God's Spirit and our spirits in open communion. Spiritually

alive, we have access to everything God's Spirit is doing, and can't be judged by unspiritual critics. Isaiah's question, 'Is there anyone around who knows God's Spirit, anyone who knows what he is doing?' has been answered: Christ knows, and we have Christ's Spirit.[3]

Paul was stating that the reality of the Spirit of God can only be found in the relationship between 'God's Spirit and our spirits': the ultimate reality of the universe is held in the communion between Father, Son, and Holy Spirit. As Paul said, 'Christ knows, and we have Christ's Spirit.' We believe that this model of 'knowing and being known' in relationship is powerful not only because it makes psychological sense but also because it echoes the way that God makes His own reality apparent to us.

Stepping out from behind our false selves (and dismantling our shadow missions) creates the conditions from which we can enter into genuine relationship and find reality. Yet, despite doing so much hard work to get to this point, many leaders will feel the strong draw of isolation. They may say:

- 'It's good to have dealt with my shame basement, but I'm not sure about getting close to people.'
- 'I'd rather keep to myself. You can't blur the lines of authority in leadership.'
- 'What if people see my vulnerability as a weakness and try to take advantage of it?'

- 'I need to be "set apart for God"; that means that I need to be alone.'

CHASING SPACES

As well as getting lost on the mountains of North Wales, I (Will) observed a fair bit of sheep farming and was always fascinated by the way the Welsh farmers could control their sheep on the rugged terrain with one sheep dog. As sheep are community animals, separating one sheep out of the flock is really challenging. Chase one sheep and invariably they all bunch up without success, but by chasing the space between the chosen sheep and the herd, the gap quickly widens and the sheep becomes isolated.[4]

In leadership, shame tends to chase the space that we already feel from others. These spaces are often the result of comparisons we have been making with leaders; that they are better communicators, more decisive, more popular, etc. The spaces can also be perceived as social isolation: the party we weren't invited to, the conference we weren't involved in. And they can be created in simple differences of personality style: when we feel a lack of connection or are misunderstood by others. These, and many other small spaces in our relationship with community, are exploited by shame. It drives into the gap, providing a catastrophic narrative as to why these spaces are apparent. Shame blames the sheep for its isolation from the community so that it not only feels alone, it also feels like that isolation is appropriate. Being separated, and believing that the separation is justified, is the primary blockage to building community and finding belonging.

Leaders are generally good at identifying and responding to obvious threats. Like Moses, we can break into a run at a moment's notice! But because shame 'chases the spaces', we are often isolated before we even realise what is going on. I very much doubt that Moses intended to isolate himself, but once he had, it took a significant intervention to get him back into relationship.

If shame has been successful in isolating us in the past, we must stay alert to any gaps in our connectedness and sense of belonging. If we fail to create new and better habits to face our insecurity, everyday leadership circumstances will inevitably provoke us to default backwards.

A popular maxim in psychology is 'Past behaviour is the most reliable predictor of future behaviour.'[5] This is primarily because humans are defensive and habitual. The lingering threat of rejection and humiliation leads to isolation (exile) unless we create new and better habits.

Andrew was not sure why he had decided to hire such a gifted young leader, but he sure did regret it. Susan had a master's degree in biblical Hebrew, and she was a brilliant communicator and wrote witty, self-effacing sermons that seemed to bring people closer to God. All he had heard for months was unceasing celebration of his recruitment skills.

Three years before, he had gone into counselling at the recommendation of the church elders. Often criticised for being emotionally inaccessible, Andrew had turned a corner and had begun to lead with greater vulnerability.

> Ironically, it was probably because of this 'new approach' that people felt able to be honest with him about how much they liked Susan.
>
> Now Andrew felt hugely insecure. To him, it was as though nobody appreciated him or could acknowledge any of the great steps he had made. He increasingly isolated himself in the office and avoided anything but the most superficial conversations about personal matters. He became critical of Susan and put her down in public, which only saw her championed even more keenly.

Brené Brown wrote, 'Shame, blame and disrespect, kill the roots from which love can grow.'[6] Andrew's default back to isolation damaged his leadership, and it also damaged his heart. He could have shared in the success of Susan's ministry and continued to grow the leadership fabric of the whole church, but instead he experienced disconnection at a heart level and a relationship breakdown with people who genuinely loved and respected him. The power of shame and isolation had killed off the roots of love in his leadership.

ISOLATION AND REALITY

Whilst occasional times of isolation can be good for you, persistent isolation reduces your ability to evaluate yourself and monitor your own decisions. If we don't trust external inputs, we receive no feedback. So, the more isolated you become, the more likely that your reality will become distorted.

In 1974, a Japanese soldier called Hiroo Onoda finally emerged from the jungle twenty-nine years after WWII had ended. The soldier had resisted several previous attempts to rescue him, including leaflet drops, because he did not trust the information he was given. It was not until Onoda's former commanding officer personally travelled to the Philippian island of Lubang to rescind his orders that Onoda finally accepted the reality that the war was over.[7]

Isolation does not necessarily mean that our worldview will become as distorted as Onoda's. However, combining insecurity with isolation can push our perspective towards the unrealistic. An isolated leader is ultimately a weak leader. They may look strong and independent, but their self-referencing judgement will let them down in the end. Isolated leaders are more likely to make negative assumptions about their colleagues or congregations than those who work collaboratively. Such leaders tend to end up refilling the shame basement and withdrawing further from belonging.

RELATE AGAINST INSTINCT

Choosing to live and lead with relationship as a priority is counter-instinctual. It is messy, time consuming, and exposing. And yet it is the key step to harness the power of belonging in your life. It is the place from which wisdom, insight, and joy in leadership all flow.

Moses' journey to letting go of his shadow mission of 'self-sufficiency' was not straightforward—one moment he seems to lead relationally and then he isolates himself again.

In Exodus 18, his father-in-law Jethro reunited the whole family in the desert and then observed how Moses was leading. He noted in verse 14, 'Why do you alone sit as judge, while all these people stand round you from morning till evening?' Moses had moved away from working relationally with Aaron and the people.

Jethro saw the impact of this isolation versus belonging and said, 'What you are doing is not good ... The work is too heavy for you; you cannot handle it alone' (verses 17–18). Moses then made a helpful change and decided to delegate. He determined to lead relationally again, despite what his instincts had been telling him.

Moses had isolated himself by setting himself up as the only one able to inform the people of 'God's decrees and instructions.'[8] Jethro's new leadership model[9] was effective and more real in the following ways:

- Leadership was disseminated amongst the Israelites
- Knowledge of the law of God was imparted to the people
- Reality was found in the threads of deeper relationship

- Moses would thrive, being less under the strain of leadership
- Belonging was celebrated across a vast leadership network
- Moses' true authority was heightened not weakened

THE RELATIONSHIP MODEL

In Moses' leadership, we have a foretaste of the leadership model used by Jesus and His followers. It is a model that consistently finds its way (perhaps by other names) into every leadership book of note. It is the reason we can say, 'The customer is always right'; because even successful people and companies can keep on learning from feedback. It is the reason why Toyota requires every new executive to work for three months on the shop floor, where the 'real' work is done.[10] It is behind habits 4, 5, and 6 of Stephen Covey's *The 7 Habits of Highly Effective People*.[11]

The apostle Paul wrote in 1 Corinthians 12 about how we are part of the 'body' of Christ. The body needs all its constituent parts to work well; though somebody once calculated that we could theoretically live without one of our two kidneys, half our liver or lungs, our spleen, gallbladder, appendix, reproductive organs, stomach, and fair chunks of our skin and brain. However, I think you would agree that the remaining 'body' would have quite a few struggles.

So, when Paul said that the eye could not say to the hand, 'I don't need you,'[12] he was not talking in biological terms, but in what worked best for a healthy whole. Surgically removing our diseased bits is technically possible, but not without consequences. All parts of our body, community, business, or church are there for a reason, and all belong.

The power of belonging is central to a Christian vision of relationship and community: every member, regardless of their gifts, vulnerabilities, or shame stories, is a part and belongs. It's a vision in which isolation is illogical.

The theology and rituals of the church draw this out:

- Within the doctrine of the Trinity, Father, Son, and Holy Spirit create completeness out of the overspill of their relationship, not out of any deficiency or need
- The celebration of Holy Communion sees all those present share in the bread and wine: this is a picture of a meal where we all share the same food as a sign of our complete unity in Christ
- The model of spiritual gifts is that a multiplicity of abilities and qualities are held in the whole, not in any individual person: the power of the church is seen in its unity, not its disunity

In an earlier chapter, we defined *belongingness* as a fundamental human value, and being in relationship with others is the practical application of this. In the seventeenth century, pastor and poet John Donne famously wrote, 'No man is an island, entire of itself.

Every man is a piece of the continent, a part of the main.'[13] Things haven't changed. Like George Berkeley's tree, things only become real when experienced in relationship.

DIVERTED BY POWER

Despite having travelled far along the journey to belonging, we are now confronted by a very real risk to our progress: the fact that relationalism poses a direct threat to the way in which we express our power. Whilst isolation is our most natural defence against un-belonging, personality power comes a close second.

Leadership requires us to exert power, and indeed this book is aimed at increasing not decreasing your power. However, this book also fundamentally challenges the way we choose to use our power. We believe that leadership power increases through working relationally, through collaboration, through training and championing others, and through disseminating praise throughout a team—from president to office cleaner. If we remain insecure, the temptation is to do the exact opposite.

Insecurity disconnects the *power* of leadership from the *purpose* of leadership. One of the most common shadow missions for leaders is 'That I might appear powerful'. They may tone it down to 'influential' or 'helpful', but what they really mean is that they are in control and other people do what they say. The power of leadership becomes an attribute to be venerated rather than a way to see this world transformed. It's a bit like celebrating the batteries of your new torch—you may have 100 watts of halogen beam, but without a path home, you're still lost.

> (Rob): I once invited an eminent speaker to address a conference I was involved in leading. From the moment we made contact, I sensed that he wanted me to be subservient to his power. Following my invitation, I received a list of specific requirements that had to be met should he agree to come. These ranged from the exact hotel he had to stay in to the precise brand of snacks required in his 'green room'. He even requested that I arrange time for him to play golf! The list itself wasn't as significant as his clear desire to wield his personality power. I decided that his presence might actually undermine other leaders and weaken the conference, and so I made my excuses and declined his requests.

The result of pursuing power is that leaders end up isolated again, but this time they are also on a pedestal. They put themselves up there, other people put them up there, and they work hard to remain up there. But pedestals are fundamentally insecure—once on top, the only way is down. Shame-based leadership is primarily underpinned by competences. Insecure leaders look to personality power, qualification, and gifting to validate their leadership. 'I am the leader because I look powerful, sound powerful, am outstanding at … (you fill in the gap).'

Personal Power or Powerful Communities

The *castellers* of the Catalan region of Spain have a tradition of building human towers that can reach over nine levels high. In a successful *castell*, the strongest people are at the bottom of the tower, unseen by the crowd and relatively uncelebrated. They let smaller and lighter people, often children, climb over them to get higher. Ultimately their leadership is celebrated in the success of the whole team, and it is the children who take the applause. This image offers the exact opposite of the model of building personal power bases that we have been exploring.

Figure 16: Power, or POWER?

The power of the castell is in the commitment of everyone to play their part, to lead in communion with others, to celebrate the vulnerable over the strong, and to help each other hold tightly. The castell is about the power of belonging, where the commitment to connectedness defines both purpose and success. The people lifting up the others are a great model of the sort of leadership habits we are proposing, and the castell itself is an excellent picture of relationalism, where what is created is real because of the real relationships between people.

There are several ways to illustrate this further, but here we give two examples—one from the organic arena of community networking and one from the boardrooms of big companies. Both show that, despite alternative ways of getting things done, the best results are seen when people are put first—which takes courage and vulnerability from those in charge.

Connected Communities

In her book *The Well-Connected Community*, Alison Gilchrist examined broken and struggling communities and put forward networking and connectivity as tools for mutual development.[14] This is sometimes called 'social capital',[15] which recognises that relationships between neighbours, colleagues, and friends have value for individuals and for society as a whole.

Human nature being what it is, communities don't always form well. They are either unstructured and lacking social capital (the new-build estates of the commuter belt give an example) or unbalanced with only some parts seeing success. It's tempting for governments to take a top-down approach and impose values, but those don't tend to work as well as the local values generated from within the community itself.

Gilchrist set out a vision for everyday citizens creating change through consensus, campaigning, and mutual action. Through these networks, trust grows and leaders remain accountable. It's informal and people rarely have titles, but changes are lasting, and people are empowered.

Levels of Leadership

In his book *The 5 Levels of Leadership*, John C. Maxwell outlined the reason certain types of leaders have influence.[16] Some lead through *position*, such as a major in the army, but this is the lowest level, as people obey you only because of leverage (you pay them, you can punish them). The next level is leading through *permission*—people let you lead because you treat them as individuals and they like you, even respect you.

Next up are those who lead through *production*—people follow you because of what you have done for the company, community, or church—and they want more of the same. This is the lowest level at which you can actually see change. The fourth level is *people development*—people follow you because of what you have done for them (personally, that is, not just for the organisation). You invest in leaders, in building people up.

The last and highest level is those who are at the *pinnacle*. They will leave a lasting legacy; they are the gurus who lead leaders. You cannot get to this level unless you consistently invest in people for the long haul.

> Moses' 'how to pick up a snake' moment was only the beginning. It was his turning point, but he had a long journey ahead of him. For much of the next twelve chapters, he clashed with God and with the Israelites. He wondered why the plagues weren't working, he faltered at the edge of the Red Sea, he struggled to provide for a hungry and lost people.
>
> But then, as we mentioned in chapter 5, in Numbers 20, Moses' shadow mission seems to finally be called out and something changes from that point on. He won a battle and let others hold his arms up, he learned to delegate, he went up a mountain and came down glowing, he dictated the Law, he destroyed the golden calf idol, he led them to the Promised Land!
>
> Powerful leadership was flowing out of him! He knew God loved him and allowed others to love him too. He was leading from a place of belonging to God and others, and seeing results!

Progressing with Relational Leadership

If you have seen the benefits of relational leadership in this chapter, we hope that you will want to take practical steps towards making this your reality. We are sure that you are already doing many of the things that we have suggested, but perhaps you weren't aware of their significance. As a result you might want to give certain activities greater priority and importance than they currently hold, whilst deciding most actively against isolationism or building a personal power base.

Invest in a Few

We need to have a small number of authentic leadership relationships in which we feel safe if we are going to have a strong belonging base to our leadership. Jesus had many relationships, but He invested very deeply in a smaller number. The 'inner circle' was the three disciples of Peter, James, and John. Then came the rest of the twelve disciples, then the seventy-two who were around them.

Peter, James, and John had an extraordinary belonging-based relationship with Jesus. He took them on special missions (Matthew 17:1), He allowed them to see His greatest glory (Mark 9:2–3) and His time of suffering in the garden of Gethsemane (Mark 14:33–34), and He prayed with them personally (Luke 9:28). They were those who saw the most of His humanity and divinity.

These three disciples became His greatest leaders after His death. He entrusted His mother to John's care. James became the first bishop of Jerusalem. Peter was called to build His church.

Take Off the Pressure

Relational leadership is more effective but also more time consuming than isolated leadership. It requires that we allow more margin in our lives to listen and to share ideas with others. It means that we need to participate in or create more forums for collaboration and idea generation. If your time is under unrelenting pressure, you will become tempted to default back into isolationism and your personal power base.

You may find that scheduling a thirty-minute 'walk about' session each day helps you to foster this relational margin. Depending on the workplace, this will differ from person to person. The intention is to have some time to strike up new conversations, build better relationships, and become more open to the leaders around you.

Speak to the Competition

In a recent Netflix drama, the role of the president of the United States is described as the loneliest job in the world.[17] There are no peers, only competitors! If we view the leaders around us simply as competitors, we get stuck in comparison making and insecurity. Inevitably we refill the shame basement and isolate ourselves against the potential humiliation of not matching up.

Decide to speak to, and even share your ideas and encouragement with, leaders that you have previously seen as competitors. Leaders who carry the power of belonging often demonstrate their security in the way that they relate to leaders who are shining brightly. Don't try to compete; see others' successes as the blessings that they are.

Have Friends Who Make Fun of You

Have good friends who aren't impressed by your leadership status. You can normally identify them as the ones who are happy to have a little joke at your expense! Friends who know you and love you beyond your leadership remind you that your value is not in what you have or will achieve, but in who you actually are.

Both of us benefit from some close friends who really care for us but aren't that interested in what we do for a living. Are you spending enough of your time investing in your real friendships, marriage, or family? Are they being left behind for the sake of your leadership? If so, reach out and restore what has been lost.

Go Anonymous

David Beckham, probably the most famous footballer in the world, set off on a two-week trek in the Amazon rainforest in 2015. As a global celebrity, he commented, 'I haven't walked through a park in 15, 20 years without being recognised, without being chased, without being photographed.'[18] In an incredible encounter with a remote Amazonian tribesman, he was asked what he did for a living.

We all need to spend time aside from our professional personas and simply be human without roles or labels. Leaders who cannot exist aside from their function of leadership will never know what it feels like to belong unconditionally.

Decide to consciously withhold your leadership position when introducing yourself to new people. Try to build relationships before your leadership role, not because of it.

Celebrate the Spiritual Dimension

A story is told that the architect Sir Christopher Wren was inspecting the building of St. Paul's Cathedral when he said to a labourer, 'What are you doing?' 'Building an arch, sir,' the labourer replied.

Unsatisfied, Wren asked another labourer, 'What are you doing?' 'Building an arch that will form part of the west door,' the man replied.

Still unsatisfied, Wren asked the stone mason working with them, 'What are you doing?' The mason turned to Wren, looked him straight in the eye, and said, 'I am building a cathedral to the glory of God, sir.' Finally, Wren was satisfied.

Physically, we may just be 'people', but our spiritual reality is that we are the body of Christ, 'living stones that are being built into a spiritual house.'[19] Relational leadership is not just more effective and powerful; it is something that has a spiritual impact. Whether we work in a secular or distinctly Christian setting, we remain members of the body of Christ. Despite the fact that we may be leading alone, we are building something far bigger than we realise.

Leading relationally without shame is a revelation of the love of God made known to us in Jesus Christ. It is a sign of a bigger spiritual truth: that we belong to God. Celebrating the spiritual reality of our leadership not only keeps us on course, it also transforms others. Belonging enables us to participate in the building of the whole cathedral—one that lives in our hearts, and in the hearts of others and in the hearts of those still to come.[20]

Figure 17: 'A Temple' by Charlie Mackesy (used with permission).

STUDY GUIDE: CHAPTER 6

Do you feel the draw of isolation, despite making progress towards belonging? If so, what is it about isolation that pulls you back?

What do you see as the challenges of relational power versus personal power? Do you long to win for the team or win for yourself?

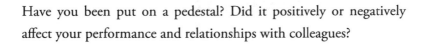

Have you been put on a pedestal? Did it positively or negatively affect your performance and relationships with colleagues?

Which of the 'steps to progress' are you already doing? Which have you decided to prioritise as a result of reading this chapter?

Chapter 7

OVERSHARING AND BELONGING BOUNDARIES

'May your life someday be as awesome as
you pretend it is on Facebook.'

Anon

(Will): Someone calls me in the office to ask what we were doing about Jane's heating. 'Her heating?' I reply. 'I thought the issue was with her stomach?' Or was it her parent's marriage, or her dog's diabetes, or her co-worker's competitiveness? These were just the issues that were current. Looking back on the preceding three years, I came to the conclusion that either Jane was the most unfortunate person I had ever met (by some significant margin), or something else was going on in her life.

Jane had leadership gifts and was highly trained in technology. She was a team leader in an international IT firm and her competences were never in question. Yet, despite this, there always seemed to be a crisis in some part of her life. Her church home group were incredibly patient and supportive, but they were beginning to struggle with the unrelenting flow of different disaster stories that dominated their attention.

Inevitably many of us took to trying to help her fix the issues that she seemed burdened by. But Jane was very reluctant to receive any support, and typically the situations seemed to gradually resolve themselves. Frustratingly, though, as soon as one crisis had ended, another began. Reflecting back on my encounters with Jane, I realise that whilst I knew a huge amount about the things in the periphery of her life—her pets or her colleagues—I knew absolutely nothing about Jane herself.

Many leaders (like Jane) could get to this point on their journey to greater belonging and say, 'I am already leading vulnerably, I share personal issues with those around me, and am always working to resolve issues relationally with others.' However true this may appear, they are in the same position as leaders who isolate themselves more obviously. Brené Brown wrote, '*Using* vulnerability is not the same thing as *being* vulnerable; it's the opposite—it's armor.'[1]

Oversharing:
- Sounds like vulnerability
- Looks like authenticity

- Tastes like collaboration
- Feels like openness
- Smells like belonging

But oversharing is just another form of self-exile. It is a more complex defence because, unlike the false self of the last chapter (which maximises our competences), oversharing displays acceptable weaknesses. Oversharing masquerades as vulnerability. Others may be flattered that we are happy to be 'authentic' with them; but what they don't realise is how contrived the material is.

Figure 18: Oversharing is still hiding.

In this chapter we will look at some of the different forms that oversharing can take. We will also offer some insights into the importance of healthy boundaries, along with some practical strategies to create genuine belonging. A wise leader once told me (Will), 'If the Devil can't get you to stop doing the right thing, he will get you to do too much of it.'

HOW NOT TO BE VULNERABLE

The difference between being vulnerable and using vulnerability is subtle but very important. We can think of reality TV 'stars' who seem unnaturally willing to share every detail about their thoughts, opinions, experiences, and passions. Despite the huge flow of personal information that is offered, there is no sense in which this makes them more authentic. Instead, we realise that their oversharing is part of a bigger attempt to influence the affection of their audiences. Oversharing in this context is often described as 'playing to the camera' and is a form of audience manipulation. Similarly, leaders who tend towards oversharing use more subtle forms than these, but they can be equally manipulative.

Leaders who withdraw tend to internalise their anxiety about being rejected, but leaders who overshare are doing the opposite; they are verbalising it. This behaviour is likely to persist because, in the short term at least, it is effective in reducing their anxiety about not being acceptable. It's only in the longer term that the behaviour can be seen for what it is (as was the case with Jane), and at that point it is very hard to change: the leader is too defended, or people are too embarrassed to confront the manipulation, and instead they just play along. Ultimately the leader's anxiety increases, apart from the fact that they are now worried about all the things they have overshared!

Below, we've outlined three classic examples of using vulnerability through oversharing (there are, of course, many others).

Sympathy Oversharing

Just like Jane, many leaders overshare a flow of carefully selected vulnerabilities to elicit the sympathy and connection of others. This isn't genuine vulnerability because the individual isn't being authentic. Instead they are using a device that keeps people close but allows themselves to remain hidden. Rather than fostering genuine belonging, the device always backfires, as people get worn out by the perpetual narrative of neediness. Rather than creating proximity, it ultimately leads to isolation.

Other leaders, particularly those who have not come to terms with their own difficult pasts, elicit sympathy by oversharing historic experiences: 'Did I tell you that I lived in six different cities before my eighth birthday? My father was in the military ...' They may share and then ask for a hug, perhaps even invading people's personal space to get one. They may tell a sad historic story in a meeting or talk with the hope of getting lots of compassionate comments afterwards.

Proactive Rejecting

Proactive rejecting is an attempt to control the rejection that a leader anticipates is coming. These leaders offer their own 'health warning' very early in a relationship along the lines of 'I will probably let you down' or 'Just so you know, I have loads of faults so don't idolise me.' They then pepper their communication with a shocking number of self-depreciating stories, all the time provoking people to reject them. They are comforted by the fact that people don't leave them, but they never feel that they really belong.

Another example is the leader who has an 'amazing testimony'— usually something about having grown up on the wrong side of the tracks and done lots of drugs or time in prison. They raise their 'old life story' at every opportunity because they still see themselves as un-belonging. They feel anxious to get their shame upfront so that they can control the rejection they are sure they will receive eventually—they don't own their shame story; their shame story owns them.

Power Oversharing

Some leaders mix the model between relational withdrawal and over-sharing. They employ social withdrawal when they are in any setting with a perceived competitor—maybe a colleague of the same level or a sibling of a similar age. They fear that people will be less than impressed with things that are meant to be impressive or might even have better ideas or be more successful leaders.

At the same time, these leaders will overshare when they sense the power balance is in their favour. They may tell grandiose or overly personal stories to younger people, students, or less experienced leaders. This power oversharing ensures that they get the buzz of belonging but without the risks necessary for a true relationship. It also poses the real risk of manipulation to audiences who are vulnerable to the interests of the oversharing leader.

IMPOSTOR BIND

The difference between using vulnerability and being vulnerable cannot be easily identified from the outside: a truly vulnerable moment might look like an overshare, or an overshare like true vulnerability. In truth, we are the only people who will know our own motives. Even if oversharing worked, it would never offer genuine belonging because *we* know it isn't real.

If we use any mechanism to elicit belonging, we concede that we truly don't belong. If the outcome appears favourable, we simply feel like an even greater impostor than before. Despite knowing this is true, mechanisms like oversharing are hard to let go of. We can find ourselves saying, like Paul, 'What I don't understand about myself is that I decide one way, but then I act another, doing things I absolutely despise.'[2]

SELF-AWARENESS AND HONEST INTENTIONS

Despite what we may think, we are not powerless to stop repeating these self-defeating behaviours of un-belonging. More importantly, God is not powerless to transform us! Olympian Eric Liddell commented, 'Circumstances may appear to wreck our lives, but God is not helpless among the ruins. God's love is still working.'[3]

The first step towards challenging these behaviours is learning greater self-awareness. If we aren't aware that we are defeating our own belonging, we cannot choose a better way. You might find that considering these five awareness questions will help you understand your oversharing better:[4]

- Am I sharing what I am actually concerned about?
- Am I looking for an emotional response or genuine help?
- Are my intentions transparent, or do I have a hidden agenda?
- Am I sharing from a position of being secure in the love of God?
- Is there a more authentic way to express myself?

Sharing because we need an emotional response is sometimes necessary, but we should consider the following:

- Is this the right setting and the right people to share this information with?
- Have I shared this information with anyone before? If so, why do I feel the need to say it again?
- Am I exercising healthy boundaries—for myself and others?
- Is my sharing in response to a sense of impending rejection or humiliation?

Evaluating our intentions through compassionate questioning is a powerful step on the journey to deeper belonging. It also creates space, not only for greater self-awareness, but also for God to bring revelation to our lives. Seeing our motivation in this new light can transform our behaviours. Rather than damaging our belonging through oversharing, we can exercise true vulnerability and build trust with a few close friends.

BELONGING BOUNDARIES

We met with a communications coach recently who stated with exasperation, 'Leaders are just so over being told to be vulnerable!' Vulnerability has become a threat to many leaders because they believe it means they are called to be a 'bleeding heart in the public square'. This is not the case, as we have made clear in the section on oversharing: vulnerability is not about inappropriately splurging your personal information in public. It is personal disclosure to a level that is appropriate to a particular relationship or setting.

Belonging-based leadership exhibits vulnerability that isn't a style of communication or sound bite; it is an inner state of security that allows for *appropriate* transparency. Audiences may hunger after greater vulnerability, but leaders can only offer vulnerability to the level that is appropriate in the given setting. Moses and Aaron exercised differing boundaries in their various settings, as brothers, and as leaders:

> Moses was alone at the burning bush, and we read he passed on 'everything' to Aaron.[5] Aaron then told 'everything' to the people of Israel. However, if we read more carefully, we see that Moses only told Aaron 'everything the LORD had sent him to say' which suggests that there was more he did

not pass on. Finding out that God had not forgotten them led the Israelites to praise Him. This was appropriate disclosure for a purpose.[6]

Boundaries enable us to discern what we share with a brother versus what we share with the nation. Henry Cloud and John Townsend's book *Boundaries* reflects, 'Boundaries define us. They define *what is me* and *what is not me*. A boundary shows me where I end and someone else begins, leading me to a sense of ownership. Knowing what I am to own and take responsibility for gives me freedom…. Taking responsibility for my life opens up many different options.'[7]

The power of belonging is expressed in our lives when we no longer feel compelled to hide our shame through isolation or oversharing; instead, we can decide to whom and to what level we will reveal our true selves. This decision is no longer made in response to the fear of humiliation, but out of a genuine desire to forge deeper and healthier relationships. When shame no longer controls your life, as Cloud says, 'You own your boundaries. They don't own you.'[8]

The three most common boundary states are:

1. Non-existent boundaries which lead us to unhealthy, co-dependent relationships and oversharing
2. Porous boundaries which lead to healthy, inter-dependent relationships and discernable vulnerability
3. Impenetrable boundaries which lead to independence from relationships and shame-based isolation

Figure 19: Non-existent boundaries, healthy boundaries, and impenetrable boundaries.

External to Internal Boundaries

(Rob): In Auckland, New Zealand, where I lived for two years, there is a very clever beacon that guides big ships down the centre of a dredged channel. As you steer directly towards it, in deep water, the light is white. If you go off to the left (port), it flashes red; and if you go off to the right (starboard), it flashes green. If you go further left, it changes to a steady red, and further right you get a steady green. This enables you to have early warnings for a wrong course and make the necessary changes. Over time, the pilots of big ships steer this channel instinctively but novice sailors like me focus on the lights all the time to navigate safely.

Boundaries are very similar to these navigation lights: they help us to discern the channel of appropriate vulnerability; whether we are too isolated or whether we are in danger of oversharing. Because the concept of 'boundaries for appropriate vulnerability' is new to many leaders, you may need to be very conscious of your external boundaries before they become more instinctual to you.

The skills needed to create good boundaries are relatively simple—choose to exercise, repeat, and practice each boundary until it becomes automatic. However, you will need perseverance with this process as we tend to go off course, at least in the early stages of implementing healthy boundaries.

1. External

Boundaries in the *external* world are typically visible to others and us. They help us to navigate our proximity to danger, from a railway crossing to how close people can stand to us. But they can also be evident in things like the organisation of your work station, diary management, and family commitments.

Some external boundaries can give us a powerful indication of our position in the channel of appropriate vulnerability. We want to encourage you to become more aware of your external boundaries: Do they foster enough opportunity for relationship or too much proximity? Do they allow people to overwhelm you, or do they work to isolate you from others? Ask yourself how your external boundaries could express your secure belonging more. Remember that you are no longer a victim of shame and that your boundaries are within your control.

2. Internal

Boundaries that are *internal* are invisible to others, but very clear to us. Internal boundaries can be stronger than external ones. One example is the ability to choose whether to accept a criticism or entertain a negative belief about ourselves. Internal boundaries help us to read subtle social clues, like the sexual interest of others, or our own complex motivations for behaviour. They can prompt us to change direction before circumstances become damaging.

Just like the experienced pilots of big ships, being conscious of the lights for long enough gives way to a more unconscious awareness of healthy boundaries. We believe that this process is not only an issue of good psychology, but also a spiritual journey. The lights of our hearts are not simply decisions that are good for us; they are the will of God for us. Developing internal boundaries is part of the process of the renewing of our minds[9] with the mind of Christ. It is wisdom.

The Volcano Model

Boundaries are not a simple set of binary (either/or) decisions. They flex and change depending on the people, setting, and pressures that we are responding to. Leadership boundaries are particularly complex and require careful discernment over what is a flexible boundary and what is an unmovable wall!

It may help you to imagine the landscape of your boundaries like a volcano[10] which rises slowly out of a plane and up to a crater. The centre of the volcano is God—and, in our model, the suggestion that He can bear everything and be told everything. You may not agree with this theologically, but a relationship with God is like any other in that it needs to be grown and built up. Disciplines of prayer, study, solitude, and worship will help with this.

You can move seamlessly from the savannah to the foothills to the slopes and then over the rim into the central pit.

We can place situations and people at various places on the volcano as shown below. There is a blurred line between where an acquaintance becomes a friend or a work event takes priority over a family one—people can move both up and down the slope. The key value of this tool is in the way it provokes us to consider how the degree of our vulnerability changes depending upon how close or far away someone or something is to the crater.

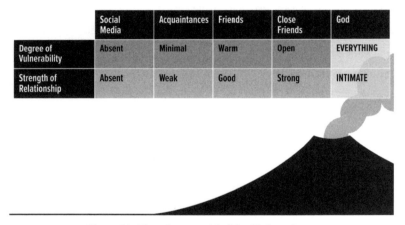

	Social Media	Acquaintances	Friends	Close Friends	God
Degree of Vulnerability	Absent	Minimal	Warm	Open	EVERYTHING
Strength of Relationship	Absent	Weak	Good	Strong	INTIMATE

Figure 20: The volcano model of flexible boundaries.

Relationship Strength

Belonging-based leaders express vulnerability in direct proportion to the strength of their relationships. This requires them to have some strong relationships and the discernment to tell them apart from the other relationships in their lives! Shame-based leaders, on the other hand, are so busy defending themselves that they struggle to discern this variance. They tend to categorise relationships into broad, simplistic groups like employees, congregations, or contacts, but fail to see how real friendship might appear at any level.

Shame-based leadership also provokes leaders to a misplaced 'equality of relationship' ideal which legitimises the shallowness of all their relationships on the basis that it is 'fair for everyone'. We want to be clear that healthy leadership is built upon a deeply unequal model of relationship, where relationships with God, spouse, family, and a small group of very close friends get a hugely disproportionate degree of vulnerability.

One discernment exercise you might try is to get one hundred coins and put them into piles on a piece of paper. Draw an X at the centre. The closeness to the centre of the paper marks the genuine strength of your relationship. The size of the pile marks the investment of time you make in that relationship.

You are allowed only one hundred coins—how are you going to divide them up? This exercise helps us see how we might reassert our boundaries to support relationships within which we can enjoy the deepest level of belonging and be the most vulnerable. As a leader, your investment of time is your greatest commodity; it can be tempting to spend it all on people who love what you do but not who you are. Do you need to consider spending more on people who love who you are, and less on people who love what you do?

Getting Help with Boundaries

Assessing and changing your boundaries is a core expression of belonging-based leadership. It is a sign that you are no longer fearful of being known, or fearful of disappointing others who might then humiliate you. The willingness to assert healthy boundaries is like raising a flag to say, 'I am at home here, and these are my house rules!'

However, this can be a challenging journey, and at times we may benefit from the wisdom of someone outside of our situation who can help us with the discernment we need to do this well. We both have found that deep and close relationships like these provide powerful ways to establish good boundaries and self-discipline.

Even if you run an independent organisation or a small business, you can find support from local networks or the Institute of Directors.[11] Likewise, there is always someone who has walked a similar path to you before and will have wrestled with boundaries issues. Even if you consider yourself a 'trailblazer', find someone who has blazed a different trail and try to hear how they have kept their boundaries healthy. It is not always easy to see our own weaknesses, and we need feedback from others. The key thing is to pick the right people and to do it in the right way. This is how authenticity is grown.

Depending on the arena within which you feel you may need help, you may want to seek the support of a coach or mentor. Here are some definitions you might find helpful:

- **Coach:** to help you to understand the external boundaries of a new setting. This might be in sport, or when you take on a management position at work. The main area of focus is on *what you can do effectively* within these boundaries. Coaching usually happens for a certain period of time and may be a formal arrangement with meetings at fixed intervals.

- **Mentor/Counsellor:** to help you explore your internal boundaries. The main focus is on *who you are*. It can be more formal and a paid arrangement, or informal and over a longer period of time, with a variety of frequencies of meetings as needed. Choosing a mentor or counsellor is more personal than choosing a coach.
- **Spiritual director:** to help you explore your spiritual boundaries. Usually focussed within a particular church tradition, but likely open to all. The aim is to deepen your relationship with Jesus, with the idea that the rest of you will follow. There will often be a number of stages on this journey, and the expectation that (in time) you may direct others.
- **Accountability groups:** these are small groups who meet regularly and intentionally to *support each other in building healthy boundaries*. Many follow an agreed set of questions each meeting but may also be flexible in approach.

(Rob): When I first became a consultant psychiatrist, I moved from being a trainee psychiatrist to being 'the lead'—the senior clinician on the team. Someone had to make the hard decisions and that someone was now me. But what if I face a really hard decision?

I was considering this when I did my first night on call—ostensibly 'in charge' of the mental health of about 300,000 people … It occurred to me, that whilst I could manage 99 percent of scenarios, there was always someone else to ask for that tricky 1 percent.

I could phone up my opposite number in the next-door city and run it by them. There was also a senior manager on call. If I really had to, I could wake up the medical director, who could wake up the chief executive. They in turn could wake up someone from the Scottish Government, who, I guess, could wake up the Queen …

I've made a habit since of sharing this with new consultants, who are always grateful and look very relieved.

An illustration used by many leadership and time-management gurus is about how lots of little things (represented by pebbles) can fill up our lives with no time for the important things (the big rocks).[12] The point of the illustration is that you need to put the big rocks in your 'jar' first, and then you will still have plenty of time, or room, for the smaller things around them.

Boundaries is one of the big rocks that we believe is essential for you to have in your jar of leadership. Accountability is another. It is amazing to us how many leaders fail to see the importance of supportive accountable relationships, or if they do, just deny that they have the space in their lives for them.

The power of belonging frees us to collaborate with others, seek accountability, and improve our boundaries. We no longer need to be defended against looking like we don't match up to the task, or fearful that we will let in the competition. Instead we can be confident in *our being* and focus on improving *our doing*.

WALKING THE VULNERABILITY TIGHTROPE

(Will): My son and I were watching some tightrope walkers travelling between two large alpine buildings in Switzerland. Joseph was absolutely mesmerised and kept asking how they stayed on the wire. It was clear that standing still was not a good long-term strategy for balance; equally, rushing forward appeared risky too. The tightrope walkers constantly adjusted their speed, sometimes stopping to reset and at other times moving forward in relatively swift motions.

Being appropriately vulnerable is a bit like walking a tightrope. The wire represents our boundaries; they help us to avoid falling to the left and into the trap of isolation or to the right and into the trap of oversharing. You might even imagine that there is an account-ability coach calling up words of encouragement from the ground below: 'Stay balanced!'

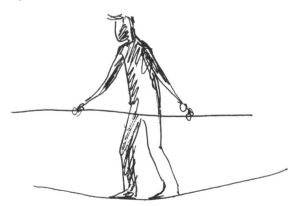

Figure 21: Appropriate vulnerability is a balance.

The vulnerability tightrope is not just about balancing between isolation and oversharing. It is also about discerning the speed at which we become more vulnerable within a relationship. In Exodus 14, Moses and the people were struggling with the balance between moving forward and standing still:

> Moses answered the people, 'Do not be afraid. Stand firm and you will see the deliverance the LORD will bring you today. The Egyptians you see today you will never see again. The LORD will fight for you; you need only to be still.' Then the LORD said to Moses, 'Why are you crying out to me? Tell the Israelites to move on.'[13]

The Israelites seemed to be facing a contradiction when, in fact, both steps work together: they needed to keep forward momentum (as the Lord was going to part the seas for their safe passage) and also be still (in heart perhaps) as the Lord would provide the wisdom for the path ahead.

Being appropriately vulnerable works along very similar lines: there is no single vulnerability speed that will guide you through your week, let alone through your life; every circumstance and relationship requires small changes to our approach. We need to keep adjusting our speed between moving forward into deeper vulnerability and being still enough to estimate relational strength. This may sound complex, but it is something you have been doing for a long time without even being conscious of it. Now that the process is not being hijacked by shame, it can serve its intended purpose and bring us into deeper, healthier relationships with others.

Posture for the Path

As we conclude this chapter, you may feel that there is a lot to consider if you are going to keep your balance as a belonging-based leader: oversharing, isolation, vulnerability, boundaries, and relational strength are all important, but the essential first step is just to get your posture right! Sonja Harpstead, a tightrope instructor in New York City, says that ultimately in tightrope walking 'posture is the absolute most important thing.'[14]

We want you to adopt the posture of leaders who truly belong and are seeking to bring others into healthy, honest, collaborative relationships. Brennan Manning invites us to this posture in his book *Abba's Child* when he says, 'Define yourself radically as one beloved by God. This is the true self. Every other identity is illusion.'[15] When we are vulnerable from a position of godly identity, our posture is one not only of great strength, but also one of great freedom. From this place our leadership is liberated; from the fear of shame to the power of belonging.

STUDY GUIDE: CHAPTER 7

Have you ever used oversharing to get something you wanted or used it to divert people from who you really are? Describe what happened.

What did you find out about yourself from the self-awareness questions in this chapter?

Which external or internal boundaries are you committed to changing as a result of reading this chapter?

Which belonging-based relationships are you determined to invest more time in?

When walking the 'vulnerability tightrope', are you more in danger of rushing forward or holding back?

Chapter 8

BEYOND BELONGING

'Aim at heaven and you will get earth thrown
in. Aim at earth and you get neither.'[1]

C. S. Lewis

The finest violins in the world are crafted from wood harvested in
the steep mountainside of the Risoud Forest, Switzerland. The best
trees for making violins are not the bristling, green spruces, as their
branches leave knots in wood which inhibits the sound. Instead, prize
wood is found in the thin, branchless trees growing in the shadow of
their healthier-looking counterparts.[2] This wood has far fewer knots
and is dryer than the lusher trees. It is the struggle of the Stradivarius
tree—the struggle for water, for light, and for space—that makes it
uniquely qualified to be crafted into a beautiful violin.

The struggle for belonging in leadership can feel very similar.
Shame has kept us locked in a forest of diminished comparisons. We
have been diverted by our shadow missions, trying to glean what we

can to match up, whilst growing in the shadows of apparently more gifted and better equipped leaders. We have looked at their resources and networks and concluded that was what we needed to flourish. But in reality no amount of resources, support, or success could have validated us because of the shame that undermined our leadership and left us feeling like impostors in our own callings.

Figure 22: The best wood in the forest is formed in the struggle for water and light.

Yet, the struggle for belonging has caused us to grow in self-awareness, compassion, vulnerability, gratitude, and confidence. So long as we continue to grasp it, our belonging is establishing our very best leadership. Rather than believing we are low-ranking trees in the shadows of the forest, God is using this struggle to transform us into a Stradivarius tree.

THE GIFT OF PAIN

The disease of leprosy, mentioned twenty-seven times in the Old and New Testaments,[3] was a feared disease, not only because there was no known cure, but because it led to total social isolation.[4] The central danger of leprosy is the damage it does to the nervous system. The aid organisation Leprosy Mission states, 'Without the gift of pain, everyday activities are fraught with danger. Unnoticed burns and ulcers can lead to permanent disability.'[5]

Following the encounter with the snake, in Exodus 4:6–7 God instructed Moses on how to perform a second sign. He was to put his hand inside his cloak and take it out again. It 'was leprous—it had become as white as snow.' He then repeated the process to restore his hand back to normal.

Perhaps even more terrifying than the snake, becoming leprous would have been a catastrophic experience for Moses. However, just like the snake, it was a sign to Moses that his shame was being called out.

There is no evidence in the text that he ever used the leprous sign with the Egyptians as he did with the snake. It is possible that he used it as a sign exclusively for the Israelites.[6] If that was the case, the significance of it would not have been lost on them: for those carrying the shame of slavery and exiled from their place of belonging, there might now be a way back.

The human mechanisms we have described in this book numb the pain of our shame: self-exile, perfectionism, the false self, competitiveness, oversharing—they all work rather too well. As a result, many leaders remain unaware of the impact of 'leading without belonging'.

Like a medical condition with no symptoms, they continue to believe that the faulty behaviours that they use to isolate themselves are doing them good: that their defensiveness is wisdom, that their sense of fraudulence is humility, and that their shadow mission is justified. Over the long term, though, shame will continue to negatively impact their leadership and their relationships.

A friend was about to undertake a 300-mile charity cycle ride in France. His company insisted that he undergo a medical check-up before he began. As a very fit and healthy man, who had no physical symptoms of illness, he assumed there would be no problem. Following a scan of his body, though, the doctors discovered a serious tumour growing inside a portion of his spine. He completed his cycle ride before having the tumour safely removed and has since made a great recovery. Without the gift of pain our friend was at huge risk; he was so grateful for the cycle ride—it literally saved his life!

Nobody enjoys pain, but seeing it as a gift can steer us away from danger and towards safety. The purpose of our writing is not that you might escape the pain of shame in your leadership but that you might become attentive to it. Following surgery for a catastrophic back injury in 2016, I (Will) was referred to a spinal physiotherapist. I had hoped he would be very sympathetic to the pain I was experiencing and maybe advise me to take more pain killers. Instead he told me, 'Listen to your pain and respond with the appropriate exercise.'

Exercising when you are in pain is totally counterintuitive and initially appeared to make things worse. However, as I followed his instructions, I noticed that not only did the pain subside over time, but my new strengthening meant that it rarely reoccurred with the same intensity. Within six months of beginning physio, I was both stronger and in less pain, but I have remained ready to respond to any recurrent pain with the right exercises.

When discomfort and fear arise in your leadership (which it will if you are taking enough godly risks!), we want to encourage you to respond to the pain, not by self-exile, but by reasserting your true belonging; choosing to lead relationally and vulnerably. We want the snake to become your staff in leadership; but that is possible only if you are willing to risk the real pain which arises from being vulnerable.

Tips for managing future pain
- Anticipate that people or circumstances will make you feel shame and rejection in leadership
- Acknowledge the pain but choose to reflect on it rather than react to it
- Share your feelings within one of your belonging-based friendships
- Decide against oversharing or isolating yourself

- Choose to continue to be appropriately vulnerable
- Reaffirm your spiritual freedom from shame
- Pray that God would strengthen your sense of belonging to Christ

DEALING WITH FUTURE REJECTION

In our experience of coaching leaders, we have learned that shame often reasserts itself through real or perceived rejection in their sphere of influence. Leadership is certainly fertile ground for insecurity and un-belonging to re-emerge. This is because the leadership setting is never solely about our personal mentality but about the leadership culture, the environment we are leading in, and ultimately the mentalities of those we are leading. Having the foresight to accommodate these challenges and respond in a way that supports belonging is key to your long-term success.

When the Culture Is Rejecting

The customs, ideas, and practices within different leadership settings vary greatly. We talk about hostile or accommodating (hard or soft) cultures as a way to describe how easy it is to integrate into them. Obviously, the hardness of a culture is both a measure of the culture itself and the difference of a particular person to it, making a leader's experience appear subjective. Different people lead well in different cultures.

The culture of a leadership setting is very hard to perceive externally; it tends to be something that we discern slowly and painfully over time. The result is that leaders often begin enthusiastically but feel exhausted and dejected as time goes on. The subtlety of cultural rejection makes a leader feel deficient rather than opposed. The result is more leader shame and un-belonging.

> Moses encountered cultural rejection in a number of subtle ways, but most apparent was the sense that he wasn't really 'one of them'. Whilst the Israelites were enslaved, Moses had lived in luxury in the Egyptian court or as a free man amongst the Midianites. The books of Exodus and Numbers always give you the impression that the Israelites were reluctant to trust in him. It is easy to sense their dismissive tone in Exodus 32:1: 'As for this fellow Moses who brought us up out of Egypt, we don't know what has happened to him.'

Cultural rejection always makes you 'this fellow' (male or female) who doesn't belong. It is also where secure personal and supernatural belonging comes into its own. Culture is never as strong as its presentation of itself, so to lead securely in a hostile culture is to enact cultural change for the better. You *can* make a difference. Three things will support your leadership:

- Secure belonging-based relationships that exist outside of the leadership culture
- An ability to identify and verbalise the cultural hostility objectively
- A 'cultural translator' (as Aaron was for Moses) to give you cultural insight

When the Environment Is Rejecting

Culture can be subtly rejecting, but environmental rejection is obvious; it shouts: 'You don't belong here' well before you have started to lead. This is manageable whilst we feel confident and secure, but the moment we waver, our leadership can begin to crumble.

> Moses led the Israelites through the Sea of Reeds and into the Desert of Shur.[7] Despite being hugely experienced in the desert country, Moses was leading in an environment which was ultimately rejecting. The Israelites in his care had walked for three days without finding water; a life-or-death matter. The first thing that they did in response to their suffering was reject his leadership: 'So the people grumbled against Moses, saying "What are we to drink?"'[8]

Insecure leadership measures itself by its ability to avoid problems, but belonging-based leadership measures up to the problems it encounters. Measuring up is not always about positive outcomes; it's about good decision making. Left to themselves, the Israelites would have returned to the slavery of Egypt several times. This would have avoided the problems of a rejecting environment, but they would have never entered the Promised Land. Moses' supernatural belonging to God enabled good leadership and ultimately provided good outcomes as God miraculously provided clean water, manna, and quails.[9]

Few of us will be leading in a desert, but we may be leading in a rejecting environment. This could be a setting which is dominated by a different person or group, and within which we feel like an obvious outsider. It could be a setting under extreme pressure, like a failing business, an overextended medical service, or a school. Your leadership will be under pressure in these settings, but the power of your belonging could make all the difference. Three things will give you the edge:

- Belong to the vision, not the problems
- Succeed by leading well, not by simplistically measuring outcomes
- Seek supernatural provision from God to whom you belong

When Others Are Rejecting

Remaining rooted in your sense of belonging is exceptionally hard when those we are seeking to lead are actively rejecting us. It is inevitable that a rejection of our leadership is felt as a rejection of us personally, and that provokes shame and un-belonging.

(Will): When I was taking over the leadership of my first church, I was still very vulnerable to a sense of un-belonging and was cautious about upsetting the existing congregation. Despite my caution, I had worked hard to design a new church website that would be the platform for communication, both within the church and to engage our local community. Having got wind of this project, a long-standing member of the church took it upon herself to call me up and give me a piece of her mind. I still remember her saying, 'You don't even know who we are so how on earth do you think that you could possibly create a website that represents us?!'

The harder I tried to placate this lady, the angrier she became. In the end we closed the call on a very dissatisfactory note and I went into a 'belonging crisis'. All of my insecurities about leadership overwhelmed me: Maybe I am not cut out for leadership. These people are going to hate me. I am going to be humiliated. I am never going to be able to get these people to listen to me. It was like a fuse had been lit in me, attached to a stick of emotional dynamite that threatened to derail my leadership altogether.

We have to become effective in our own self-talk in the light of the leadership rejection of others. 'What lies behind us and what lies before us are small matters compared to what lies within us.'[10] It is this internal reaction between what lies within us and other people's rejection of us that makes for such an explosive result. Separating these two elements from each other nearly always restores our sense of security as people who belong.

Amazingly, the woman who called Will that day went on to become a good friend and loyal supporter of his ministry. Her manner was just unusually direct! What he had taken to be abject rejection was just her normal mode of disagreement.

Here are three things that will give you perspective when you are rejected by others:

- Recognise that it is rarely you whom they are rejecting
- See your belonging as existing beyond the individual or group
- Let your secure leadership vindicate you over time, and remember your past competence

MOSES' LATE LEADERSHIP REJECTION

Moses' leadership experience with the Israelites would be blighted by rejection, despite him having liberated them from four hundred years of slavery. At the same time, we see a belonging-based leadership growing within Moses throughout the Israelites' journey to Canaan. In Numbers 14 we pick up the story:

'The people cried all night and complained to Moses and Aaron, "We wish we had died in Egypt or somewhere out here in the desert! Is the LORD leading us into Canaan, just to have us killed and our women and children captured? We'd be better off in Egypt." Then they said to one another, "Let's choose our own leader and go back.""[11]

Having brought them this far, it must have wounded Moses to hear those last words. Certainly, the Moses we met in Exodus 4 would probably have taken this as confirmation that his leadership was over. However, rather than reacting with insecurity or anger, he pleaded with the Lord for mercy on the people, 'You are merciful, and you treat people better than they deserve. So please forgive these people, just as you have forgiven them ever since they left Egypt.'[12]

Moses demonstrated how belonging releases compassion. He came to know who he was as a leader because of it. When he eventually died, we read that he 'knew the Lord face to face'[13] and there was no prophet like him. A similar type of compassion is seen in Jesus, who was able to plea for His persecutors and those who scorned Him.[14]

The prophet Isaiah foretold a man who 'was despised and rejected by mankind, a man of suffering, and familiar with pain ... we held him in low esteem.'[15] In the context of the ultimate rejection, Jesus exercised the perfect form of the power of belonging—healing the sick, raising the dead, and casting out demons. Even death could not hold this back.

Whether we are leading in a rejecting culture or a rejecting environment, or amongst rejecting people, the power of belonging can enable us to lead well. Jesus was the ultimate 'radical belonger' whose identity was so secure in God that He could face the worst possible rejection and still love others rather than serve Himself. We can share in this.

SHARING IN THE OTHER TRACK

Within our Christian faith there are things that only God can do (like save us), things only we can do (like invite Him in), and things that we can only do together (like be church). The journey to belonging is not dissimilar: only we can choose to be vulnerable, and only together can we experience belonging-based relationships. But only God can supernaturally overcome shame in the world!

We have spent much of the preceding chapters exploring things that only we can do (alone or with others) to overcome shame and find belonging. Psychology has a great deal to teach us in this regard.

However, 'radical belongers' are people who have an even greater security. This sort of belonging is more profound than a human decision for vulnerability or the determination to risk humiliation, (though these decisions still need to be made). This sort of belonging can only be received from God Himself.

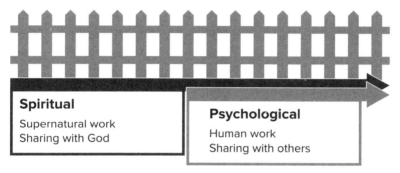

Figure 23: The two tracks of belonging.

Divine Work with Shame

God has done a supernatural work with shame that forms the second track of recovery. Looking back at the garden of Eden (home) as described in Genesis 2, it was a place of complete belonging for Adam and Eve, who were naked yet felt no shame. (Their nakedness could be understood as a position of complete vulnerability for us.)

The snake sowed mistrust into the promises of God, and Adam and Eve broke God's boundaries, became aware of their nakedness, and were ashamed. They were then exiled from the garden and hid themselves with coverings (not unlike our false selves). As Pope John Paul II said, 'At that moment shame reaches its deepest level and seems to shake the foundations of their existence.'[16]

The rest of the Bible tells the story of God's victory over shame and our return from exile to the home of heaven.

After Eden

God turned the snake into a staff for Moses (a prophetic sign of that shame and exile would give way to restoration). Then the Israelites came across venomous snakes in the desert, and many died.[17] God told Moses to make a bronze snake and raise it up on a pole so that anyone afflicted might look up and receive healing (a prophetic sign of God's rescue in Jesus).

The New Testament then completes this journey. John wrote, 'As Moses lifted up the bronze snake on a pole in the wilderness, so the Son of Man must be lifted up.'[18] On the cross Jesus became our shame (the snake) so that we might become the righteousness of God.

At His crucifixion ('lifting up'), we are told that the temple curtain was torn in two.[19] This curtain divided the Holy of Holies (God's presence) from the rest of the temple (the people). Shame was overcome, exile was over, and now mankind and God are united again in a belonging-based relationship and heaven (the new Eden) is our home.

The Church

Jesus established the church order so that we might have a foretaste of 'home' now and fulfil the mission of the kingdom of God. Church is the place where our supernatural belonging to God is experienced in relationship to other people, where we can be 'the body of Christ'.[20] It is also the place from which we can bring the hope of supernatural belonging to an isolated and shame-bound world.

TWO HOPES

In a part of South Devon, where I (Will) love to surf, are two tiny villages called Inner Hope and Outer Hope. They are separated only by a small rocky headland. If you are walking up the costal path, you cannot get to Outer Hope unless you have gone through Inner Hope. Until the 1970s, despite being neighbours, Inner Hope belonged in a different district, but now the tiny villages have been merged and together are known as Hope Cove.

Imagine that all the psychological and human exercises for belonging we have described are Outer Hope. They can exist on their own and be very useful to your leadership. They provide the hope of leading in a more secure and confident manner, where you recognise you belong and no longer feel like an impostor. Other people also directly connect with your *Outer Hope* and respond to your leadership in a more connected and honouring manner.

Imagine the supernatural work of God in Jesus, to overcome shame and exile, restoring us to our true belonging as sons and daughters in Him, is *Inner Hope*. It gives you a deeper confidence altogether which exists despite all the rejecting experiences that we have described above. Our *Inner Hope* cannot be shaken because it is the work of God. We can simply keep accepting that we belong to Him as a daily decision.

To merge *Inner Hope* and *Outer Hope* into a unified response against shame and un-belonging is to find the true power of belonging. When we exercise *Outer Hope* with the confidence of our *Inner Hope*, we have a security that is very hard to shake. Paul made this explicit in Romans 5:5 when he said, 'Hope does not put us to shame, because God's love has been poured out into our hearts through the Holy Spirit, who has been given to us.'

THE DECISION TO KEEP ON TRACK

It's possible to be a secure, belonging-based leader without knowing the supernatural belonging that Jesus offers. But we believe that the spiritual track tells us the 'why' that explains the psychological track's 'how'. Also, these two tracks reinforce each other, and when they do, something very profound occurs in our leadership. The power of our supernatural security in Christ supercharges the courage we have to lead, not to appease.

Shame can undo our resolve to lead vulnerably in subtle ways. We want to encourage you to harness the power of making bold, practical, and spiritual decisions to stay on track. Certainly reading this book will help you, but if you leave it gathering dust on your bookshelf along with its core principles, your shame basement may slowly refill! Belonging is both a state of grace and a statement of decision. Every day will be filled with opportunities to hide our true selves, placate others, and live like impostors; these are the same opportunities we have to exercise authority, be appropriately vulnerable, collaborate, and champion others. We need to decide which opportunity we are going to take. Our decisions:

(Will): I am determined to keep 'showing up'—meaning that I will be myself and not wear a mask. In fact, I have got a bit of a reputation for awkward levels of honesty. This isn't because I am naturally courageous, far from it—I have an anxiety disorder! I am simply making the determined practical steps to demonstrate my supernatural reality. My daily shaving mirror prayer is, 'God, let me fear You today and not man.' As I meditate on my belonging to Christ, my practical leadership remains secure, and as I determine to lead securely, my spiritual reality feels more real to me.

(Rob): I am sometimes asked if, as a psychiatrist, I can read people's minds. It's tempting to say, 'Yes,' but the truth is that no human can do this. Even colleagues of mine who do full-time therapy are no more than intuitive. Part of the change in therapy comes from the therapist 'showing up' in a similar kind of way—to say things that are often unsaid, to be themselves rather than a cardboard cut-out or 'super-therapist'. I need to know myself very well—and I believe this means spiritual knowledge too. Every day I decide to lead as Rob, knowing that I belong to God and am at home within my professional sphere.

BELONGING AND LEADING

As we conclude this journey, we want to make a call to radical action in a world that is awash with rejection and un-belonging.

In C. S. Lewis' Narnia tale *The Voyage of the Dawn Treader*, after struggling through many trials, four (now secure) heroes stand at the very edge of the world.[21] Where next? What next? The four characters go separate but appropriate ways. Radical belonging liberates us to lead aside from the constraints of others' approval. It is the beginning of a new adventure in leadership.

As Christian leaders, we have an opportunity to make an impact on the lives of those in our care, to stay on course for God's true mission in our lives: We can make a difference—through strategic, compassionate, and secure leadership; leadership that belongs to vision more than popularity and people more than commodity, leadership that is supernaturally underpinned by our radical belonging to God through the death and resurrection life of Jesus Christ. As Paul said, 'Be joyful in hope, patient in affliction, faithful in prayer.'[22]

What does your leadership adventure look like from here?

Figure 24: Staff in hand and ready for a new adventure in leadership.

STUDY GUIDE: CHAPTER 8

In what ways do you think the struggle for belonging has actually been a blessing to your leadership?

How will you respond to the 'gift of pain' in future encounters with leadership rejection?

Have you experienced Inner Hope? If not, are you willing to explore how God can transform your experience of shame?

Which decisions have you made to ensure that you don't allow the shame basement to refill? How will you respond to opportunities to be appropriately vulnerable in leadership?

What does your next great adventure in leadership look like?

APPENDIX

THE SHAME BASEMENT MEDITATION

You approach a small door in a wall, the padlock is rusted and brittle. You feel nervous as you put a key in the lock, not because the door won't open, but because it will. You are tempted to walk away, but you sense that God is calling you forward.

You make your way down steep stone steps into the basement below. The walls are lined with photographs, but these aren't happy occasions. They are the memories that you have buried out of sight; moments of rejection, embarrassment, and humiliation. They are the reason you have not let anybody in here before. These pictures hang like a judgement over your life, accusing you of being unacceptable, unredeemable, and ultimately unlovable.

You move slowly past them and into the darkest corner of the basement floor. In the gloom you can see an old stained sheet hanging limply over a trunk. You feel your heart beating faster as you consider which horrible memories might be locked within. Again, you are tempted to retreat back up the steps, but you slowly pull back the cloth. It falls to the ground and you notice that it is stained with blood, as if a body had once been wrapped within.

You grip the side of the heavy lid and lift it back against the wall. Light floods the basement, pictures that hung in judgement against you immediately fade, unrecognisable in your sight. You turn your eyes to the contents of the trunk. It is filled with the pictures that you didn't take, pictures that line the mind of God and others. Each one contains you—loved, held, comforted, comforting, holding, loving. These are the images of your belonging.

There are no trophies, no certificates, and no prizes in this box. There is nothing that recognises your achievements, or your lack of achievements. Everything within shows a love you cannot work for, one that you can only receive. Inside the lid is a written note: 'Because I first loved you.'

The basement is no longer a hostile place. Its door is always open to you and even to a few trusted friends. You go down the stone steps whenever you need to be reminded that 'you belong'; that the power you carry to lead is not built on your performance but on love.

PRAYERS
A Prayer When Threatened by Humiliation

'Dear Lord, I feel afraid that I am about to be humiliated. Being exposed as a failure in front of others fills me with dread and I am tempted to withdraw from the risk and isolate myself. I know that You are with me, that You love me. I pray that You will come and meet me in my fear. I choose to stand on the truth that You are greater than my darkest fear: that my authority and leadership is rooted in my belonging to You. Help me to keep my eyes fixed on You so that I can stand my ground regardless of the risks. I stand on Your promise "never to leave me or forsake me." In Jesus' name, amen.'

A Prayer for the Courage to Be Yourself

'Lord God, You are my refuge and my strength. You have called me to be courageous, not to live in fear of what people think about me. I know You are calling me to step away from my false self and shadow mission. Strengthen me as I seek to live a life of integrity without partition. Give me the courage to be appropriately vulnerable and the wisdom to discern who can support me on this journey. When I face criticism or rejection, help me to remain secure in my belonging to You and my community. Every day give me the determination to seek Your will over my desire to please or placate others. Father, today, give me the courage to be myself and to lead in the knowledge that in Your strength I am strong. In Jesus' name, amen.'

A Prayer for a Deeper Sense of Belonging

'Father God, I have struggled to believe that I belong aside from my usefulness. I realise that my security has become dependent upon my own achievements. You have called me into leadership, and I know that You are equipping me for the call on my life. Fill me with a security that comes from being Your child. Help me understand the depths of Your love for me, despite my faults and failings. Help me to lead from a place of secure belonging, recognising that my value does not come from my achievements but from who You say that I am. For Christ's sake, amen.'

A Prayer for When Shame Rises Up

'Jesus, when You went to the cross I know that You dealt with shame once and for all. You became my shame so that I might be made righteous. I want to thank You for what You have done for me and I receive the truth of Your victory over death and sin into my life again today. You have promised that "I will not be put to shame" and I trust You beyond the shame that I feel today. I receive Your words of love and compassion, that my identity is as a child of God. I choose the truth of Your Word over the lies of the enemy. I invite Your Holy Spirit to fill me afresh today, driving away the shadows of my shame and filling me with the presence of God. In Your precious name, amen.'

COMFORTING VERSES FOR TIMES OF CHALLENGE

Galatians 5:1 'It is for freedom that Christ has set us free. Stand firm, then, and do not let yourselves be burdened again by a yoke of slavery.'

Isaiah 61:7 'Instead of your shame you will receive a double portion, and instead of disgrace you will rejoice in your inheritance. And so you will inherit a double portion in your land, and everlasting joy will be yours.'

Psalm 56:3–4 'When I am afraid, I put my trust in you. In God, whose word I praise—in God I trust and am not afraid. What can mere mortals do to me?'

Mark 9:41 'Truly I tell you, anyone who gives you a cup of water in my name because you belong to the Messiah will certainly not lose their reward.'

Deuteronomy 31:6 'Be strong and courageous. Do not be afraid or terrified because of them, for the Lord your God goes with you; he will never leave you nor forsake you.'

2 Corinthians 12:9 'But he said to me, "My grace is sufficient for you, for my power is made perfect in weakness." Therefore, I will boast all the more gladly about my weaknesses, so that Christ's power may rest on me.'

Isaiah 54:4 'Do not be afraid; you will not be put to shame. Do not fear disgrace; you will not be humiliated.'

Romans 5:5–6 'Hope does not disappoint us, because God has poured out His love into our hearts through the Holy Spirit, whom He has given us. For at just the right time, while we were still powerless, Christ died for the ungodly.'

2 Timothy 1:7 'For the Spirit God gave us does not make us timid, but gives us power, love and self-discipline.'

1 John 4:4 NLT 'But you belong to God, my dear children. You have already won a victory over those people, because the Spirit who lives in you is greater than the spirit who lives in the world.'

WHEN SELF-ATTACKING THOUGHTS COME IN

When we are wrestling with shame and the fear of un-belonging, self-attacking or catastrophic thoughts may intrude into your mind. We call these ANTs: automatic negative thoughts.

They might include thoughts like, *If people really knew me, they would all reject me. You have failed again and you are going to be exposed. You are unlovable and a fraud.* ANTs are very attention grabbing and initiate a chain reaction of possibilities which ultimately lead us to a place of catastrophic fear.

Catastrophising is underpinned by two important beliefs:

1. The unreasonable belief that the worst *will definitely* happen
2. The unreasonable belief that you won't be able to cope when it does

Catastrophising can seem quite irrational when we hear someone else describe their thoughts, but when we are in the fear spiral, it feels very real and is deeply distressing. Shame-bound leaders describe their daily experience as being an unrelenting walk through the scariest possibilities imaginable.

Forewarned Is Forearmed?

Some people are more dispositioned towards catastrophising than others, which is probably linked to their anxiety levels, as the whole process has an intended protective function. *Praemonitus, praemunitus,*' roughly translates to 'Forewarned is forearmed,' showing that this proverb has been around for a lot longer than the five hundred years it has been in English print.

Catastrophising is the mind's way of forewarning you of circumstances that could lead to your rejection or humiliation. In truth, every healthy mind provides this function. If you are standing next to a bonfire, you may visualise yourself being burned as a protective function. The issue with catastrophising is the lack of bonfire, and the extreme and convoluted journey between stimulus and destination.

When we scrutinise it, 'Forewarned is forearmed' is limited wisdom. The fire may be hot, but you could not predict tripping and falling into it. Cancer is dangerous, but you cannot stop it from appearing by worrying about it. Terrorism is a possibility but not a predictable one. The point is, forewarning rarely protects us from reality; if anything it just leaves us living in a haze of anxious discomfort.

Rumination, escalation, and low confidence all fuel the power of this process: Rumination is the process of overthinking and exploring threats. Escalation is in unwarranted magnification of these threats and their probability. Low confidence is important because it leaves the individual believing that they would be unable to cope with the outcome should it occur. Ironically, these three elements spiral into each other to keep the cycle alive. The less I (Will) believe I can cope with rejection, the more threatening the situation appears and the greater it escalates!

Not Getting on the Train

Imagine your mind is like a railway station and the trains are thoughts that stop at your platform. The first step to recovery is to accept that you cannot stop the trains from arriving and opening their doors to you. In fact, attempts to do this (suppression, repression, or denial) usually lead to even more frequent and scary thoughts.

Whilst you cannot stop the trains from arriving at your platform, you can decide not to get on board when they open their doors to you. I use the tube in London every week. Multiple trains arrive at Earl's Court that have different destinations despite there being just two tracks. It is a discipline to resist the urge just to jump on board any train that arrives and sit down, but if you do, you are probably going to end up in the wrong part of London.

Catastrophic thoughts tend to have a very strong draw about them. After all, they usually present themselves as life-or-death matters! The result is that we tend to 'jump on that train' straight away without thinking about the destination. With catastrophising, the destination is never resolution, clarity, and reassurance; it is despair, confusion, and more terrifying shame-based thoughts!

Stay Calm and Aware

Mindful awareness is simply the process of remaining on the platform and allowing the thought train to leave without you on board. I find it helpful to label these thoughts with a casual detachment, 'Oh, look, there's my "You're a fraud."' Or, 'There is the "You are going to mess everything up and get totally humiliated" thought.' Somehow by labelling the thought, our minds are more able to observe but not engage these rogue threats, and the good news is, the more practiced we become, the easier it gets.

Dealing with catastrophising is hard work, but you can make progress. If you feel uncomfortable at first, you are doing the right thing; persistence is key to winning, so keep working at it every time you feel tempted to begin ruminating again. Always remember that you are stronger than you think—even if the worst did happen, you could cope with it.

SEEKING HELP FROM OTHERS

For some people, the journey from shame to belonging can be complex and provoke difficult feelings. Shame also acts to block people from receiving the support that they need, because it makes emotional challenges feel like a weakness. Remember that receiving support for your emotions is no different from receiving support when you become physically unwell. Speaking to someone else can help you maintain the progress you have already made and further improve your emotional health.

Seeing a Pastor

Discussing your journey away from shame and into belonging enables the empathy of others to dissolve your fear of rejection. A trusted pastor, who will listen in a non-judgemental way, can be a really helpful person on your journey of recovery. It may be that this person will be able to offer you ongoing encouragement within the context of the church family and seek to affirm you within your leadership roles there.

Seeing a Counsellor

A trained counsellor or therapist can help you in a number of ways: They can be a sounding board and provide a focussed space each week for your thoughts. They can help you overcome internal barriers and defences. They can give you specific techniques if you have times of more severe depression or anxiety.

The most important thing is to find a good counsellor. Look for someone who is accredited by one of the main national counselling organisations. This may cost you some money, but it will probably be worth it. You may want someone who shares your faith, but it is more important to see someone who is well qualified. A good counsellor will respect your faith and not seek to undermine it.

Seeing a Doctor

For extended periods of painful emotions, it may be advisable to see a doctor. This can be your GP (general practitioner) or family physician in the first instance. They may suggest you see a psychiatrist as well. It could be that treatment of a depressive illness (or similar) is necessary to fully complete your journey.

This is not saying anything about the depth of your faith—this is a medical issue arising from the way some people's brains work. Remember, if you begin to feel unsafe or at risk in any way, you should seek urgent help from your local health services.

FURTHER RESOURCES

To access more resources about the power of belonging, including video, audio, and supporting articles, go to:

www.mindandsoulfoundation.org/belonging

The Mind and Soul Foundation website is also your gateway to over 100 audio and video resources and over 500 articles on the whole area of Christianity and emotional health, including other books by Will and Rob. Supported by active social media accounts and conferencing, it is the world's largest resource on this topic.

NOTES

INTRODUCTION

1. Naomi Reed, *No Ordinary View: A Season of Faith and Mission in the Himalayas* (Milton Keynes, England: Authentic, 2008).

2. *Journal of Behavioral Science*, cited in Danielle Page, 'How Impostor Syndrome Is Holding You Back at Work', NBC News, 25 October 2017, www.nbcnews.com /better/health/how-impostor-syndrome-holding-you-back-work-ncna814231.

3. Kirsten Weir, 'Feel Like a Fraud?', American Psychological Association, November 2013, www.apa.org/gradpsych/2013/11/fraud.aspx.

4. Whilst it is not necessary to be a Christian to have a sense of belonging, we believe that this is ultimately where belonging finds its own home. For many shame-bound leaders, God is distant—a figure of awe, or a strict headmaster. However, the Bible is full of descriptions of God as someone who walks alongside us and, being the Risen Lord, has walked this journey Himself already and knows its end.

CHAPTER 1: LONGING FOR HOME

1. Maya Angelou, *All God's Children Need Travelling Shoes* (New York: Random, 1991), 196. This is the fifth book in Maya Angelou's seven-volume autobiography. Like all the books, it continues her story as an African American woman coming to terms with her family's narrative of slavery and wondering where

'home' is. Is it back in Africa near her ancestors, or by becoming assimilated into the American culture which enslaved them?

2. Kent Hoffman, et al., 'Changing Toddlers' and Preschoolers' Attachment Classifications: The Circle of Security Intervention', *Journal of Consulting and Clinical Psychology* 74, no. 6 (2006): 1017–26.

3. 'Hamilton: I Couldn't Have Done It without My Team', Grand Prix 247, 6 September 2015, www.grandprix247.com/2015/09/06/hamilton-i-couldnt-have -done-it-without-my-team/ (emphasis added).

4. *C. G. Jung: The Collected Works*, vol. 26, ed. Herbert Read, Michael Fordham, and Gerhard Adler, trans. R. F. C. Hull (New York: Routledge, 2014), 7322.

5. Please note, we have nothing against the sharing of tasty-looking food or even kitten videos. These have their place. We do, however, have an issue when this sharing is done to generate 'likes' to boost a faltering self-esteem.

6. See Exodus 2.

7. *Ubuntu* is the word Tutu uses to describe his theology where forgiveness is pos- sible because of relationships. See 'Ubuntu Theology', Wikipedia, accessed 19 July 2018, www.wikipedia.org/wiki/Ubuntu_theology for more information.

8. Desmond Tutu, *No Future without Forgiveness* (London: Rider, 2000), 35.

9. Julianne Holt-Lunstad, Timothy Smith, and J. Bradley Layton, 'Social Relationships and Mortality Risk: A Meta-analytic Review', *PLOS Medicine* 7, no. 7 (27 July 2010): e1000316.

10. I (Rob) have written a blog post on this called 'Solitude and Being Alone' which starts with the quote 'Jesus calls us from loneliness to solitude' from Richard Foster's book *Celebration of Discipline* (New York: Harper Collins, 2002). Read the blog post at www.mindandsoulfoundation.org/Articles/195414/Mind_and _Soul/Articles/Solitude_and_being.aspx.

11. Danielle Page, 'How Impostor Syndrome Is Holding You Back at Work', NBC News, 25 October 2017, www.nbcnews.com/better/health/how-impostor -syndrome-holding-you-back-work-ncna814231.

12. Jesus discusses this explicitly in John 3:1–15. This is the classic 'born again' passage after which evangelical Christians are often known. However, we only get half the meaning if we think Nicodemus was just making a biological point about being unable to fit into a uterus again. He knew Jesus had God 'with him' and wished the same closeness, the same belonging. He got the metaphor of

returning to that infantile state of connection, so he asked if it were possible and marvelled (ESV) at the idea.

13. *Summer in the Forest*, directed by Randall Wright (R2W Films, 2016).

14. Jean Vanier, *From Brokenness to Community* (New York: Paulist Press, 1992), 35.

15. For example, in Luke 8:56, Jesus raised Jairus' daughter from the dead and the text reports, 'Her parents were astonished, but he ordered them not to tell anyone what had happened.'

16. Matthew 27:12 NLT.

17. Matthew 3:17; 1 Corinthians 15:27; Revelation 5:6.

CHAPTER 2: BELONGINGNESS

1. Brené Brown, *The Gifts of Imperfection: Let Go of Who You Think You're Supposed to Be and Embrace Who You Are* (Center City, MN: Hazelden, 2010), 40.

2. A. H. Maslow, 'A Theory of Human Motivation', *Psychological Review* 50, no. 4 (1943): 370–96. You can find a readable and fairly accurate introduction on Wikipedia.

3. Roy F. Baumeister and Mark R. Leary, 'The Need to Belong: Desire for Interpersonal Attachments as a Fundamental Human Motivation', *Psychological Bulletin* 117, no. 3 (1995): 497–529.

4. See Revelation 21:10.

5. The nation of Israel is replaced by the *diaspora* (Greek: διασπορά). Many of the later New Testament letters are addressed to these people—the dispersed believers in and near various Mediterranean cities.

6. Nicky Gumbel, Clergy Leadership Training, Holy Trinity Brompton, March 2018.

7. Philippians 3:20.

8. Revelation 21:3–4.

9. John 14:2.

10. An old Lutheran hymn starts with the words 'I'm but a stranger here, Heaven is my home; Earth is but a desert drear, Heaven is my home.' Contrast this with the Randy Newman classic called 'Heaven Is My Home' which is all

about how having a future in heaven motivates you to help a friend down here right now.

11. Robin Williams, in *World's Greatest Dad*, directed by Bobcat Goldthwait (Dallas: Magnolia, 2009).

12. *The Prince of Egypt*, directed by Brenda Chapman (Universal City, CA: DreamWorks, 1998).

13. Gershen Kaufman, *The Psychology of Shame: Theory and Treatment of Shame-Based Conditions* (New York: Springer, 1989), 5.

CHAPTER 3: UNDERSTANDING SHAME

1. Brené Brown, *Braving the Wilderness: The Quest for True Belonging and the Courage to Stand Alone* (London: Vermillion, 2017), 32.

2. Rachel E. Jack, Oliver G. B. Garrod, and Philippe G. Schyns, 'Dynamic Facial Expressions of Emotion Transmit an Evolving Hierarchy of Signals over Time', *Current Biology*, 2 January 2014, www.cell.com/current-biology/fulltext/S0960 -9822(13)01519-4.

3. Silvan S. Tomkins, *Affect, Imagery, and Consciousness Volume 2: The Negative Affects* (New York: Springer, 1963).

4. Social anxiety disorder is a medical condition about which a lot is known. See more information at www.nhs.uk/conditions/social-anxiety. The treatment of choice is cognitive behavioural therapy (CBT) which is available through the National Health Service and many private providers. If you think you have social anxiety which limits your performance, you should see your GP.

5. Rick Hanson and Rick Mendius, 'From Shame to Worth', Wellspring, 8 January 2018, www.wisebrain.org/wortharticle.pdf.

6. This model is a simplified depiction of various psychoanalytical theories about shame (see the next endnote for a list). You can think of this like a tree, with roots and shoots, or you can think of it like a Ferrero Rocher chocolate—a squishy middle of insecurity bound up in a gooey mass of toffee and covered with a brittle chocolate shell.

7. Shame has been looked at extensively in psychoanalytical literature by analysts such as Léon Wurmser, Andrew P. Morrison, Phil Mollon, and Sidney Levin. Many of the academic papers are hard to read with complex psychoanalytical

terminology, but there are some more accessible books on the subject from this perspective.

8. S. Levin, 'Some Metaphysical Considerations on the Differentiation Between Shame and Guilt', *International Journal of Psycho-Analysis* 48 (1967): 267–76.

9. As an interesting aside, anthropologist Ruth Benedict (*The Chrysanthemum and the Sword*, 2006) proposed that cultures are classified by whether they use shame or guilt to regulate behaviour. Traditionally, Western cultures are seen as guilt based and Eastern cultures are more shame based. However, it is our hypothesis that shame is alive and well in Western cultures, especially considering the role it plays in limiting leadership potential.

10. Online Etymology Dictionary, s.v. 'shame', accessed 19 July 2018, www.etymonline.com/word/Shame.

11. For a more detailed discussion on the role of shame as 'super-ego functions' that serve as regulators of drives, see H. B. Lewis, 'Shame and Guilt in Neurosis', *Psychoanalytic Review* 58, no. 3 (1971): 419–38, esp. 422–23.

12. Exodus 2:14.

13. Ronald Potter-Efron and Patricia Potter-Efron, *Letting Go of Shame: Understanding How Shame Affects Your Life* (Center City, MN: Hazelden, 1989), 14.

14. Carl Gustav Jung was a contemporary of Sigmund Freud and the founder of the modern school of analytical psychology. See C. H. Mayer, 'Shame—"A Soul Feeding Emotion": Archetypal Work and the Transformation of the Shadow of Shame in a Group Development Process', in *The Value of Shame*, ed. E. Vanderheiden and C. H. Mayer (Cham, Switzerland: Springer, 2017), 277–302.

15. Please note that shame stories, by definition, are shameful and so just 'opening up' about them is unlikely to be helpful. A skilled therapist can help you tell your story in the context of a supportive and secure relationship. We will discuss this more in later chapters.

16. Brennan Manning, *Abba's Child: The Cry of the Heart for Intimate Belonging* (Colorado Springs: Navpress, 2015), 12.

CHAPTER 4: HOW TO PICK UP A SNAKE

1. Thucydides (Greek historian, 471–400 BC). This quote is from II.43 from his 'Funeral Oration' given by Pericles who had just led the Athenians into the Peloponnesian war.

2. Exodus 4:2–4.

3. Sigmund Freud, 'Remembering, Repeating and Working Through (Further Recommendations in the Technique of Psychoanalysis II)' (1914), 12:145–56.

4. Brené Brown, *Daring Greatly: How the Courage to Be Vulnerable Transforms the Way We Live, Love, Parent, and Lead* (New York: Avery, 2012).

5. The Uraeus (usually a cobra or asp) was a symbol of sovereignty, royalty, deity, and divine authority in ancient Egypt. See www.wikipedia.org/wiki/Uraeus for more details.

6. John Wesley, *Commentary on the Whole Bible* (1754–1765), accessed 19 July 2018, www.biblestudytools.com/commentaries/wesleys-explanatory-notes/exodus/exodus-4.html.

7. John Wesley, preface to *Explanatory Notes upon the Old Testament* (1755). See Craig L. Adams, 'What John Wesley Actually Said About the Bible', Commonplace Holiness, February 2012, www.craigladams.com/archive/files/john-wesley-on-the-bible.html for more information.

8. Rev. Stephen Foster, sermon at Holy Trinity Brompton, London, 15 October 2017.

9. Exodus 3:5–6.

CHAPTER 5: SECURITY AND SUCCESS

1. 'Vin Diesel: I Want to Be a Good Dad', *Parade*, 25 August 2008, https://parade.com/32179/parade/pc_0230/.

2. Anna Freud, *The Ego and The Mechanisms of Defense* (originally published in German in 1936), trans. Cecil Baines (New York: Routledge, 1937, 2018).

3. Abraham Maslow, 'The Dynamics of Psychological Security-Insecurity', *Journal of Personality* 10, no. 4 (1942): 331–44.

4. Bill Johnson, sermon at Bethel Church, Redding, California, 26 February 2014.

5. Brian A. Primack, et al., 'Social Media Use and Perceived Social Isolation Among Young Adults in the U.S.', *American Journal of Preventive Medicine* 53, no. 1 (July 2017): 1–8, www.ajpmonline.org/article/S0749-3797(17)30016-8/fulltext.

6. Thomas Merton, *New Seeds of Contemplation* (New York: New Directions, 1961), 34.

7. Walter Scott, *Marmion: A Tale of Flodden Field* (Edinburgh: Ballantyne, 1808), canto VI, XVII.

8. John Ortberg, *Overcoming Your Shadow Mission* (Grand Rapids, MI: Zondervan, 2008), 27.

9. Ortberg, *Overcoming Your Shadow Mission*, 9.

10. Ortberg, *Overcoming Your Shadow Mission*, 27.

11. There is a good Wikipedia article about this at www.wikipedia.org/wiki/Hero%27s _journey. You can also read more specifically about how this 'monomyth' underlies many movies at www.movieoutline.com/articles/the-hero-journey-mythic -structure-of-joseph-campbell-monomyth.html.

12. We've called these stages 'signposts' because they are waymarkers by which you can navigate. For more information on how these signposts and landmarks are used in the Ignatian tradition (which is the basis of much spiritual direction) see: Margaret Silf, *Landmarks: Exploration of Ignatian Spirituality* (London: Darton, Longman & Todd, 1998).

13. Matthew 11:28 The Message.

CHAPTER 6: RELATIONALISM

1. Bishop and philosopher George Berkeley (1685–1753). For an overview of George Berkeley's philosophical ideas, see http://philosophyforyou.tripod.com /berkeley.html.

2. George Berkeley was the main proponent of immaterialism or subjective idealism. Relationalism is closely related to this and attributed to the Indian philosopher Joseph Kaipayil. For those who want to get into the philosophy, it's important to remember that we can (a) get overly into relationalism and say that we can never truly know anything about anything because we are always relating to anything we are studying and hence affecting it, or (b) be overly anti- and abstract and say that things just are and our perspective doesn't matter—a viewpoint called materialism. Instead, our point is that all of us cannot be isolated islands, but we are to exist within relationships and the wider society.

3. 1 Corinthians 2:14–16 The Message.

4. I (Will) credit Dr. Robi Sonderegger with the 'Chasing the gap' principle, as I heard the concept in one of his lectures.

5. Gordon Livingston, *Too Soon Old, Too Late Smart: Thirty True Things You Need to Know* (Philadelphia: Da Capo, 2008), 8.

6. Brené Brown, *The Gifts of Imperfection: Let Go of Who You Think You're Supposed to Be and Embrace Who You Are* (Center City, MN: Hazelden, 2010).

7. 'Japan WW2 Solider Who Refused to Surrender Hiroo Onoda Dies', BBC News, 17 January 2014, www.bbc.co.uk/news/world-asia-25772192.

8. Exodus 18:15.

9. Exodus 18:23–26.

10. See the following overview article as to why the Toyota production system works—not as a set of ideas and tools, but as an overarching approach to how things work. Steven Spear, 'Learning to Lead at Toyota', *Harvard Business Review*, May 2004, https://hbr.org/2004/05/learning-to-lead-at-toyota.

11. Stephen R. Covey, *The 7 Habits of Highly Successful People* (New York: Simon and Schuster, 1989).

12. 1 Corinthians 12:21.

13. John Donne, *Devotions upon Emergent Occasions* (1624).

14. Alison Gilchrist, *The Well-Connected Community: A Networking Approach to Community Development*, 2nd edition (Bristol: Policy, 2009).

15. A term introduced by L. J. Hanifan in school reform over a century ago. Hanifan, 'The Rural School Community Center', *The Annals of the American Academy of Political and Social Science* 67 (September 1916): 130–38.

16. John C. Maxwell, *The 5 Levels of Leadership: Proven Steps to Maximize Your Potential* (New York: Center Street, 2011).

17. *Designated Survivor*, episode 14, 'Commander-in-Chief', directed by Frederick E. O. Toye, written by David Guggenheim, Michael Gunn, aired 29 March 2017, on Netflix.

18. David Beckham, quoted in Holden Frith, 'Into the Unknown: David Beckham's Motorcycle Diary', *The Week*, 10 June 2014, www.theweek.co.uk/tv -radio/58905/into-the-unknown-david-beckham-s-motorcycle-diary.

19. 1 Peter 2:5.

20. The phrase 'cathedral in your heart' is expounded by pastor and speaker Paul Scanlon as investing in dreams that will not benefit you. As he said, 'Planting trees under whose shade you will never sit.' It is a vision built on an under-standing of relationships and the power they have to go beyond us. Leaders on

pedestals can't think this way. See and hear more at https://paulscanlon.com /cathedral-in-your-heart/.

CHAPTER 7: OVERSHARING AND BELONGING BOUNDARIES

1. Brené Brown, *Daring Greatly: How the Courage to Be Vulnerable Transforms the Way We Live, Love, Parent, and Lead* (New York: Avery, 2012).

2. Romans 7:14–16 The Message.

3. Eric Liddell, quoted in *The Goal and The Glory: World-Class Athletes Share Their Inspiring Stories* (Ventura, CA: Regal, 2008), 130.

4. A longer list of questions is available at www.becomingwhoyouare.net/vulnerability -vs-over-sharing-where-to-draw-the-line/.

5. Exodus 4:28.

6. Exodus 4:30–31.

7. Henry Cloud and John Townsend, *Boundaries: When to Say Yes, How to Say No, to Take Control of Your Life* (Grand Rapids, MI: Zondervan, 1992), 31.

8. Cloud and Townsend, *Boundaries*, 124.

9. Romans 12:2.

10. This is our own model. There are a number of extensions you can consider; for example, people can move up and down the slopes of the volcano as they become closer or drift away. Sometimes people are just friends for a season. You can also consider what would happen if the volcano moved across the plane. Real volcanoes don't do that, of course, but we do change as we get older, and our views and priorities change too.

11. The Institute of Directors will be found in many countries—see www.gndi.org for one list, though there are others. They support and educate directors and board members in many sizes of company. We are not saying that they are perfect, or that they are your boss, but our point is that there is always someone to ask.

12. One humorous example of this can be seen on YouTube featuring Stephen Covey at www.youtube.com/watch?v=ciBRcrOgFJU.

13. Exodus 14:13–15.

14. Katie Nodjimbadem, 'What Happens to Your Body When You Walk on a Tightrope?', Smithsonian.com, 13 October 2015, www.smithsonianmag.com /science-nature/what-happens-your-body-when-you-walk-tightrope-180956897 /#IgGDdz2ARmFZZPU5.99.

15. Brennan Manning, *Abba's Child: The Cry of the Heart for Intimate Belonging* (Colorado Springs: Navpress, 2015).

CHAPTER 8: BEYOND BELONGING

1. C. S. Lewis, *Mere Christianity* (Grand Rapids, MI: Zondervan, 1941).

2. John Laurenson, 'Switzerland's "Violin Trees"—Looking for the Perfect Wood', DW, 23 April 2013, www.dw.com/en/switzerlands-violin-trees-looking-for-the -perfect-wood/a-16762187.

3. Biblegateway.com s.v. 'leprosy', word search, accessed 20 July 2018, www.biblegateway.com/quicksearch/?quicksearch=leprosy.

4. Leviticus 13:8 says, 'The priest is to examine that person, and if the rash has spread in the skin, he shall pronounce them unclean; it is a defiling skin disease.' Even though leprosy is not that infectious, it was similar to other skin diseases that were, and people were made to live apart.

5. 'What Is Leprosy?', The Leprosy Mission England and Wales, accessed 20 July 2018, www.leprosymission.org.uk/about-us-and-leprosy/what-is-leprosy/.

6. See Exodus 4:30 where it is recorded that Moses 'did the signs.'

7. Exodus 15:22–24.

8. Exodus 15:24.

9. See Exodus 15:25 and Exodus 16.

10. *Meditations in Wall Street* (New York: William Morrow, 1940), 131.

11. Numbers 14:1–4.

12. Numbers 14:19.

13. Deuteronomy 34:10–12.

14. Luke 23:33–34.

15. Isaiah 53:3.

16. Quoted in Christopher West, *Theology of the Body Explained: A Commentary on John Paul II's 'Gospel of the Body'* (Leominster: Gracewing, 2003), 145.

17. Numbers 21.

18. John 3:14 NLT.

19. Matthew 27:51.

20. 1 Corinthians 12:27.

21. C. S. Lewis, *The Voyage of the Dawn Treader* (London: Harper Collins, 1952).

22. Romans 12:12.